PAUL AND HIS CONVERTS

PAUL AND HIS CONVERTS

The Sprunt Lectures 1985

ERNEST BEST

T & T CLARK
EDINBURGH

Copyright © T. & T. Clark Ltd, 1988
Typeset by Saxon Printing Ltd, Derby,
printed and bound by Billing and Sons Ltd, Worcester

for

T. & T. CLARK LTD,
59 George Street, Edinburgh EH 2 2LQ

First Printed 1988

British Library Cataloguing in Publication Data

Best, Ernest
Paul and his Converts.
1. Paul, *the Apostle*
I. Title
225.9'24 BS2506

ISBN 0-567-09147-3 (cased)
0-567-09147-2 (paperback)

CONTENTS

ABBREVIATIONS

G.N.B. Good News Bible
J.S.N.T. Journal for the Study of the New Testament
J.T.S. Journal of Theological Studies
L.C.L. Loeb Classical Library
N.E.B. New English Bible
N.T.S. New Testament Studies
R.S.V. Revised Standard Version
T.D.N.T. Theological Dictionary of the New Testament

PREFACE

The occasion of this book was the gracious invitation from Union Theological Seminary, Richmond, Virginia, to deliver the 1985 Sprunt Lectures. I am both honoured to have been invited and indebted to the faculty for the kind way in which they received me, in particular to Professor and Mrs Rissi who took care of all the entertainment of myself and my wife.

The choice of subject was dictated by the type of audience, mainly pastors on active duty for whom a purely academic approach might not have related to their work. A number of factors led to the particular area within a possible wide field. I had written commentaries on I and II Thessalonians and on II Corinthians which are among the most pastorally oriented of Paul's letters. I had been approached by a publisher about the re-issue of a book on Paul as pastor which had first appeared at the beginning of this century. I did not recommend its re-issue since Pauline studies have changed so much in the period but in reading it I realised that here was a field that had not been explored recently as a whole, though studies of particular areas within it are now beginning to appear. In this way I settled on my subject. The structure of lecture series dictates that there should always be five lectures. Unfortunately Paul did not always organise his material to suit this pattern and so the original five lectures now appear as eight chapters.

Though it was not my main purpose to provide a picture of Paul in these lectures it was inevitable that one would appear, and one drawn from a less usual angle. The result has been a portrait in which many of the 'warts' which books on Paul's theology do not observe or treat show up. The theoretical expression of one's beliefs may not necessarily reflect personal character. Perhaps some who read this will object to certain aspects of this picture of Paul. Let them recollect that Paul was not without sin and that what emerges here is not the whole Paul. Neither his missionary work nor his intellectual understanding of Christianity are considered. An evaluation of these needs to be added to that of his pastoral care if Paul is to be seen as he really was.

I

MODELS

Introduction

These lectures deal with the relation between Paul and the churches he founded as it is displayed in his letters to them. How did he view his relation to them and their relation to him? Under what models did he present himself? How did he counsel, advise and instruct them? How did he treat those he thought were perverting his work? In his pastoral activity did he remain faithful to his main theological position? Did he deal with his converts in the way he advised them to deal with one another? I shall not in these lectures be attempting to sketch Paul's theology, his missionary activity or his personal faith. Enough has been written in these areas. Instead my approach will be from a less usual direction and I hope this may open up his rich and many-sided character afresh. Of the three major areas of his work, pioneer missionary, theologian and pastor, it is the last which has received least attention.

If we approach Paul from the angle of his pastoral work this does not mean that we have to accept him as either the perfect pastor or the model for modern pastors. There is much to learn from him, yet there are quite a number of reasons why he cannot be taken in any simple and straightforward way as model. In the first place all pastoral work belongs to particular situations. That is why visiting preachers often do not relate sympathetically with the congregations to which they minister in one day stands. Coming in as visitors they are unaware of the total pastoral context. Secondly, the pastoral contexts of congregations in western civilisation are very different from those with which Paul had to deal. We do not need to spend time advising our hearers about buying or not buying meat in

1

the local store because it may have been sacrificed to an idol before being put on sale. We are much more aware of the problem of sexual equality between men and women than was the culture of Paul's day. While in every church there will be some who expect that the Lord will return soon they do not allow this to dominate their lives; they insure themselves against ill-health, accident and old age; they do not give up their jobs as some of Paul's converts did (2 Thess. 3.6-13).

As a person Paul differed from most of us, and the way he dealt with others stemmed at least partly from the kind of person he was. Reared in a hellenistic-jewish culture he received a top-level Jewish education so that he learned to think in particular ways. To argue in the way he did about Sarah and Hagar (Gal. 4.21-31) came naturally to him though it might not to us. That he was a man capable of very strong views is seen in the way he persecuted believers before he became one himself. When he became a Christian he did not lose his ability to hold his views strongly. We know by looking at pastors as they work that their characters affect the way they behave. Faced with a difficult situation one will act instinctively and jump in; another will mull the situation over and only then make a move. Paul's character must have affected the way he carried out his pastoral work.

Three possible ways of acting were open to Paul when he encountered a problem. He could write a letter, send one of his team, perhaps Timothy or Titus (2 Cor. 8.16-17; 1 Cor. 4.17), or himself visit the church (1 Cor. 11.34). Unfortunately we have no direct reports of what happened when he adopted one of the latter two courses; all our information comes from his letters. For all practical purposes we are therefore restricted to these. That in itself brings out other aspects of the difference between Paul's pastoral situation and ours. Almost all our work is carried out face to face, or perhaps mouth to ear on the telephone. It is unusual for us to act by means of letter. We normally counsel individuals; Paul counselled whole churches. Those we counsel are close at hand; those Paul counselled were often hundreds of miles away. Without telephones there was no up-to-date information and a visitor from another church might not be a reliable reporter. If Paul's reaction to certain situations seems obscure let us remember the situation may have seemed obscure to him, and yet he felt he had to say something. Other obvious differences exist between a minister or priest today and Paul. No denominational body placed him in charge of his congregations. He was also always responsible for a number of churches and not given the oversight of only one. He had to keep in touch simultaneously with several, and these were geographically distant from one another and could not be visited in the course of a single day.

Before we go further it is necessary to explain the phrase 'pastoral situation'. Its use is not intended to limit what follows to those who are professional pastors. Every Christian lives in a pastoral situation as parent, sibling, teacher, employer, lawyer, union official, team captain. Thus what we learn from Paul if it has any value for ourselves has value not only for those we call 'pastors' but for all who believe.

Our Sources
Those who write about Paul have necessarily to define which of the letters attributed to him they believe he actually wrote. With most scholars I assume he did not write the Pastorals (1 and 2 Timothy, Titus). Even if they were accepted as genuine they would not be of much help to us since they were not written to counsel churches but individual pastors. Again the majority of scholars would not accept Colossians and Ephesians as genuine; however these in any case lie outside the area of relevant material for we are inquiring into the way Paul treated the churches he founded and he did not found the churches to which these letters are written (see Col. 1.4; 2.1;

Eph. 1.15; 3.2; 4.20-21). For a very similar reason we have to leave aside what many regard as Paul's greatest letter, that to the church at Rome. This church was in existence many years before he wrote; a few of its members may have been his converts in other cities who had later moved to Rome and joined that church but the majority of its members had become Christians through the efforts of other evangelists.[1] We are then left with 1 and 2 Corinthians, Galatians, Philippians,[2] 1 and 2 Thessalonians (I take the second letter to be as much by Paul as the first[3]) and Philemon.

Some scholars have doubted if Paul converted Philemon. In v. 19 he says Philemon owes his very self to him (i.e. Paul). On the face of it this would suggest he was Paul's convert. But might he not have been such indirectly, a convert of one of Paul's converts or of one of his team? [4] However as Guthrie [5] comments the whole letter is 'too intimate to be a letter to a stranger'. It is also doubtful if the point Paul is making (receive back Onesimus because you owe me a debt) would be nearly as effective if Philemon were not Paul's direct convert. Although Paul never evangelized Colossae where Philemon apparently lived the latter may have met him in Ephesus during Paul's long stay there and been converted; Philemon as a man of some wealth (he owned slaves) would have been able to travel. As we proceed with our examination of Paul's pastoral work with his undoubted converts we shall see that the way he treats Philemon does not differ from the way he treats other converts. Justification for our conclusion that Philemon was his convert will lie in the end result of what we do.

As we have said Paul did not write Romans to converts; for this reason it forms a useful control to see if his pastoral approach to his own converts and churches differed in any way from that to those who were not. We shall see that there are significant variations in the two approaches.[6]

We need also to take note of the one speech in Acts where Paul addresses converts (more correctly, leaders of one of his churches, who will of course have been his converts).[7] According to Acts 20.17 Paul summoned the elders of the church of Ephesus to meet him in Miletus. Most scholars consider that the author of Acts in accordance with contemporary historical practice composed the book's speeches; this speech then, though it may contain Pauline tradition cannot be traced back to Paul. Even if we reject this conclusion and argue instead that Luke was present at its delivery (20.18-35 falls within one of the so-called 'we-passages') there are still considerable difficulties in our utilisation of the speech. It is inconceivable that Paul should put the Ephesian elders to the necessity of a long journey to Miletus and then only speak to them for the five minutes that the speech would take.[8] What we have can then at best be only a summary. As such it certainly indicates in broad terms Paul's care for his churches; this adds nothing to what we learn from his letters. As a summary it cannot be used as an accurate source for the detailed understanding of terms and concepts. Anyone who has summarised a speech or article of someone else knows how easy it is to encapsulate the thought of a passage in a word or phrase which has not actually been used in the original. This is particularly so if the summary is made at a later period. The writer might well employ words and images which were prevalent in the later period but had not been used by the speaker although they would adequately express his meaning. So Luke could have taken up the shepherd imagery to express Paul's pastoral care though Paul himself never used it in his letters.[9] Indeed the letters we term the Pastorals do not use pastoral imagery but the term is a good description of them. Given then that the best we can hope for is that we have a summary of the original it is difficult to use the speech, though it must be said there is nothing in it which stands as exceptional in comparison with

5

the genuine letters to converts, except perhaps the prophecy about the future of the church (20.29-30). As we deal with the material from the letters we shall point out differences and similarities with the speech.[10] There will naturally be some differences caused by the situation of the speech as one of 'farewell' for in none of his letters does Paul inform his readers that he will never see them again.

The Wider Situation

Paul was an evangelist and theologian as well as a pastor and we cannot assume there was no tension between these roles. In 2 Cor. 2.12,13 he tells us he was preaching in Troas where God had opened a door for him to evangelise. Yet he suddenly pulled out from a thriving missionary situation to dash across into Europe to see if he could find Titus whom he had sent to Corinth to clear up a very difficult situation; he could have no peace of mind until he found out if Titus had succeeded in his task. Ought he not to have had that inner peace in Christ (Phil. 4.6-7) which would have allowed him to forget the situation in Corinth? We cannot answer that but we can observe the tension of the situation. All his pastoral letters were indeed written while he was heavily engaged in evangelism, under the pressures of a situation different from that to which he was writing, and at the same time he was working to support himself.

If we cannot isolate the work of Paul as pastor from the total area of his work no more can we separate Paul and his converts from the world in which they lived and regard them as a closed circle. Both he and they were affected by all that went on around them. They in particular continued to feel the pressures of the pagan environment to which they had once wholly belonged. This created endless problems, with many of which Paul deals in his letters. But problems were also created by other Christians. There was much coming and going between the young Christian communities. Incoming Christians might introduce ideas and practices differing from those Paul had taught his converts and so cause confusion. Their relationship with him might then be disturbed. In some of his letters he deals with such problems. Paul himself had continually to be looking over his shoulder at what might be happening in other parts of the church, in particular as to what Peter and James might be saying and doing. He had also to take account of the activities of his associates of whom some like Silas and Apollos were not even his converts. Even those closest to us can sometimes inadvertently mess up our plans.

If Paul had to keep a watchful eye on Peter, James and his associates he is also always looking, as we might say, upwards to Christ. The Christ whom he met on the Damascus road remained as real a person to him as Timothy or Peter. In all his relationships with others there is then always a third party, Christ, God or the Spirit. The presence of this third party continually affects his treatment of his converts. If he looked upwards he had also, as it were, to look downwards to Satan. He was real to him and could be blamed for at least some of his trials (2 Cor. 11.14; 12.7; 1 Thess. 2.18).

Paul's Pastoral Aim

What Paul was attempting to do in his letters can be summed up in the reason he gives for sending Timothy to Thessalonica, 'to establish you in your faith and to exhort you' (1 Thess. 3.2). At 1 Thess. 3.10 he says he prays earnestly to see them so that he may supply what is lacking in their faith. At 5.11 he directs the Thessalonians to 'encourage one another and build one another up'; this could equally describe his own work for he adds 'just as we are doing.' His approach was never spiritual in the narrow sense for as he prayed for those same Thessalonians that their 'spirit and soul and body' might be found 'sound and blameless' at the return of Christ (5.23) so he himself set out to

7

meet the needs of the whole person. He was concerned about the poor of the church in Jerusalem.[11] The gifts of the Spirit he hoped to see in his converts included those of administration (Rom. 12.6-8; 1 Cor. 12.28). If his approach was not narrowly spiritual neither was it narrowly intellectual though he often meets his converts at an intellectual level because many of their problems required clear thinking for their resolution. Again he was not primarily concerned to calm them down when they were excited and distraught but to speak the truth and encourage them to do God's will.

Paul Himself

I have yet to hear a preacher say to his congregation 'Imitate me.' The theme of most is 'Don't do as I do, but do as I say.' Paul however had no hesitation in instructing his converts to imitate him (1 Cor. 4.16; 11.1; Phil. 3.17). If this demand of Paul does not amaze us it ought to; we shall return to it in Chapter III. For the moment we note that it appears to give Paul a unique position. There is much which suggests the same.

Did he not claim to be the last to have seen the risen Christ?[12] This is the gist of 1 Cor. 15.3-10. He begins there with a list of those who had seen the risen Lord, not a list of those who had a genuine and continuing fellowship with him (countless millions of Christians have enjoyed the latter). He instances Peter, the Twelve, the five hundred brethren, James and the apostles. Then finally he adds himself 'last of all ... to me.' To emphasise this he picks up a word which probably had been used about him by his critics, 'one untimely born',[13] for he had never been a disciple of the earthly Jesus. If someone believed he or she were the last to have seen the risen Jesus and that no one else would ever see him again would that not lead that person to think he or she occupied a unique place in the history of the church? If Paul thought like that it should not surprise us that he calls on others to imitate him. Acts also testifies to the

8

uniqueness of Paul in this respect for no one else in Acts is converted by an appearance of the exalted Christ. Incidentally this is another reason for not taking Paul in any simple fashion as a pattern for pastoral activity: he became a pastor in a very different way from everyone else.

The same isolated position that he allocates to himself appears in his claim to have a special apostolate to the Gentiles (Rom. 1.1-6; 11.13).[14] He makes no allowance for the fact that he was not the first to take the Gospel to them (Peter had preceded him in evangelizing Cornelius, Acts 10.1 - 11.18) or that there had been a Gentile mission before his work began (Acts 11.19-26). He did not found the church in Rome which was largely Gentile. He and Barnabas had worked alongside one another in the Gentile mission (Acts chaps 13,14; Gal. 2.1,9). When they split there is no reason to suppose that Barnabas ceased to work among Gentiles (Acts 15.39). Yet Paul believed himself to be *the* apostle to the Gentiles.

The distinctiveness he felt about himself appears also in the way he believes he received his gospel. It did not come from men nor was he taught it by them; it came through a revelation of Jesus Christ (Gal. 1.1,11-12). It is possible that Paul even envisaged himself as possessing atoning significance for his converts. In 1 Cor. 4.9-13 he sketches a picture of his own life which could well be a sketch of that of Jesus and goes on to describe himself as 'refuse' (*perikatharmata*) and 'offscouring' (*peripsēma*), words that sometimes carry a redemptive connotation.[15] If this were so it would at once set up a unique bond between Paul and his converts; unfortunately the evidence is not sufficently strong to permit us to offer a positive evaluation.

There is a much simpler way however in which he views his own fate as linked to that of his converts. The reward he will eventually receive as a good master builder (1 Cor. 3.10-15) will depend on the way what he builds endures, i.e. on the lives

9

lived by his converts. On the day of judgement they will, or will not, be his joy and crown (1 Thess. 2.19,20; Phil. 4.1). How they have lived will show whether he has run or laboured in vain (Phil. 2.16; cf also 1 Cor. 9.1b-2; 2 Cor. 3.2-3). It is he who has betrothed his converts to Christ and he alone who will present them to him in the final judgement (2 Cor. 11.1-3). Yet Apollos and others have laboured over them and guided them in the faith.

To return to Paul's possible feeling of uniqueness. There were other factors which may have contributed to it. On one occasion he had a most unusual spiritual experience of which he had never spoken to anyone until fourteen years after it had taken place and then only because his authority was being challenged. The experience was that of a vision in which he was transported into the third heaven. There he saw things which he was neither able nor permitted to communicate (2 Cor. 12.2-5). In a lesser way he was marked out from most of the other Christian leaders by being the only one who was a Roman citizen and probably by being born with a silver spoon in his mouth as the son of at least reasonably wealthy parents. He was the bright young lad who had made it from Tarsus to Jerusalem where he had had the finest of Jewish educations. Again unlike the other leaders he had once persecuted the faith to which he now adhered. He had persecuted it with every possible enthusiasm; now he threw himself into missionary work with the same enthusiasm so that he could boast that he worked harder than any of them (1 Cor. 15.10).

If these were factors which made Paul different from the other leaders of the church there were also those which made him different from the vast majority of his converts. He was a Jew, they were Gentiles. Passages where he indicates the superiority of Jews as God's people over Gentiles show how much he valued his birth (Rom. 3.1-2; 9.3-5), even if at the same time his mind persuaded him that both Jew and Gentile stood on the same plane before God in needing his grace. The picture he draws of the pagan world in Rom. 1.18-32 (cf 1 Cor. 6.9-11) is not that of the careful observer but of the Jewish apologist; the Gentile world was never as bad as Paul depicts it. With his Judaeo-Christian morality and his horror of idolatry he knew where Gentiles, and therefore his converts, would go wrong and he had a base from which he could launch attacks to correct them. We shall see more of this when we look at his converts.

Before we do so it will be no harm to point out some differences between Paul and missionaries of our day. The latter almost invariably move from the culture in which they were brought up into a new and strange culture. Paul had not however grown up in a culture alien to that in which he later worked. He did not leave an area of high technology to work among primitive peasants. Tarsus was in no way unique among Greek cities. He was not in any way worried by the problem of colour and only by that of race in so far as he had to free himself from the belief that his own was superior. Language was no barrier as he moved around the ancient world; speaking Greek he would be understood everywhere. Many then of the obstacles facing the modern missionary did not exist for Paul.

The Converts
In order to explore the relation between Paul and his converts it is as important to understand them as it is to understand him. They came from a diversity of backgrounds, almost all of them very different from that of Paul himself. They had gone through very different experiences when becoming Christians. None of them had met the risen Christ whether on the road to Damascus or on that from Corinth to Cenchreae. None of them, so far as we know, had ever persecuted the church before being converted. They were his converts in a way that he would never have allowed he was anyone's. Generally speaking we have no descriptions of their conversions apart from the few,

11

and it is a few, which Acts provides. Paul never finds a need to remind them how they were converted; they themselves know and it is sufficent for him to work from the fact itself. Probably the only possible generalisation to be made is that none of them were brought up in Christian homes. Conversion meant for all of them a rapid transition from a pagan culture to a Judaeo-Christian.

Growing up as a Jew Paul would have been accustomed to continuous scorn of the heathen and their gods. He was in no danger of entering a pagan temple, except perhaps for sightseeing and he did not have much time for that, in still less danger of worshipping the gods therein. But his mainly Gentile converts were accustomed to an atmosphere in which many gods were worshipped. It was not always easy for them to grasp that their new faith did not simply mean adding another god to those they already worshipped, none of whom would have jealously objected to the addition of Jesus to their number. Paul's converts had not only to grasp the exclusiveness of their new God but they had also to face the practical problems that were thereby produced. Was it right to buy meat in the market-place if the meat had previously formed part of a pagan sacrifice? Was it proper to eat it if it was served in a friend's house?

Other changes in attitude were necessary. Jewish morality, the foundation of Paul's morality, held a rigorous view of sex. So we find Paul dealing with questions of incest, the resort to prostitutes and divorce (1 Corinthians chaps 5-7). Paul would not have held that Jews were perfect in the way they behaved but unlike Gentiles they at least knew what God demanded (Rom. 2.17-18,23). The guidelines of pagan morality, and it would be wrong to say there were none, were very different from those of Christianity; Paul had both to teach new guidelines and to exhort his converts to live by them. When converts were instructed to abandon the old guidelines and accept the new they were naturally destabilized for a period.

Last century when missionaries introduced Christianity into new areas old cultural patterns collapsed without the immediate creation of new stable societies. The problem of course would not have been as great for Paul as for the modern missionary for his converts were in no danger of associating technological advance with Christianity. Yet there was the danger of continuing to fear the power of the old gods whom they believed had once controlled their lives. Were they still subject to fate, destiny, luck, the movement of the stars? Would magic still affect them if used by friends and relatives to lure them back to the old ways? And the old ways still lay enticingly around.

Looked at from a social and economic angle rather than a religious Paul's converts turn out to be much more of a mixed bag.[16] They may all have come from pagan society but that society was itself divided between rich and poor, educated and uneducated. There were independent and semi-independent shopkeepers and tradesmen, paid employees and unpaid slaves, and there were the well-to-do. The early church has often been depicted as if it consisted solely of the lower classes and slaves. This is a false inference from 1 Cor. 1.26 with its assertion that there were not many Christians who were educated, powerful or nobly born. There is no reason to dispute this. But if any random group in contemporary society had been examined the same would have been found to be true. There were simply not many in the ancient world who were educated, powerful or nobly born. There is nothing to suggest that the Christian community was in this respect anything other than a normal cross-section of society. We have to be careful in drawing deductions. It would be wrong to conclude that because Paul sometimes uses sophisticated intellectual arguments that therefore his converts were all well educated.[17] It is not unknown for preachers to talk above the heads of their people (cf. 2 Pet. 3.16).

13

There were certainly rich and influential people in the church. Some had houses large enough for the holding of church gatherings (1 Cor. 16.19; Col. 4.15; Rom. 16.5; Acts 18.7);[18] some were wealthy enough to own slaves (Philm 15,16); some held positions of importance in the wider community (Rom. 16.23; Acts 13.12; 17.12,34). Even the slaves in the church were not those of the great rural estates who were little better than agricultural animals or machines; Christianity at this time was an urban movement and many of the slaves would have been well-educated, holding positions of responsibility within their households.

Coming then from a variety of socio-economic background but in almost every case from pagan society Paul's converts were very different from those who in the beginning had entered the church from Judaism. Contact between the two groups would naturally produce stress and strain. Not all Christians of Jewish stock took the same position as Paul in relation to the admission of Gentiles to the church; when these encountered Gentile Christians difficulties and even divisions might appear. Such difficulties and divisions created problems for Paul as he dealt with his converts.

Paul of course had a relation with others than his converts through the latter. Naturally he influenced the general outside world through them but in a much more intense way he affected their immediate families, for he regards pagan wives as brought into the holy people through their Christian husbands and pagan husbands through their wives and the children through one or other Christian parent (l Cor. 7.14-16). When Paul writes to one of his congregations we must assume he has these people in mind as well as his direct converts.

We do not know the size of the congregations to which Paul wrote. Probably meetings of all the Christians in a city were unusual (1 Cor. 14.23; Rom. 16.23). Normally the church would meet as a number of groups in the houses of its wealthier members.[19] Archeological excavations show that at any rate in Corinth these would not have held more than thirty or forty people, at most fifty.[20] Separate house churches might lead to churches developing in different directions, perhaps leading to the groups Paul indicates as existing in Corinth (1 Cor. 1.11-13). If meals including the eucharist were celebrated in private homes this might lead to social division (1 Cor.11.17-22).[21] The well-to-do would have reclined with the owner and his family in the dining room (the *triclinium*) while the remainder would have sat in the courtyard (the *atrium*). It would have been difficult under such circumstances to preserve privacy. A notice could not be hung on the house door:

Religious Service in Progress

Please Keep Out.

Someone might casually enter and this may explain the peculiar reference to the attitude of outsiders to tongues and prophecy (1 Cor. 14.23-25). There is no indication at any point that non-Christian members of the household should be excluded while the service was going on. We may assume the household was treated as a unit and as Christian if its head was a Christian (see 1 Cor. 7.14-16 and the references to the baptisms of complete households in Acts 16.15, 33).

Models of behaviour

How we treat people depends both on what we think of them and our objective in dealing with them. Colonial officials may regard the tribes under their administration as consisting of uncivilised natives who will never change and their main duty as the preservation of law and order so that their district may yield good profits for the colonial power. Other seemingly more enlightened officials may look paternalistically on the natives and envisage their task as that of leading them slowly to civilisation, which does not mean they would necessarily regard them as their equals. This illustrates the issue. Paul of

15

course was in no danger of behaving as a colonial official for he was not appointed by any government. Moreover he was not dealing with a group of ignorant natives with skins a different colour from his own. In terms of wealth and education many to whom he preached were his equals, if not his superiors. He could not then assume a high-handed attitude. His sole superiority lay in his understanding of God and his Christ, in his grasp of the nature of true morality and in his attitude to idolatry and what went with it. But with these we must also couple his character and the nature of the groups into which his converts were formed if we are to determine what attitude he would take up towards them.

We begin then with what he believed to be the nature of the communities he founded. Each little group had been won from the powers of darkness and needed to be continually preserved from slipping back under their control. Its members had been delivered from this present evil age but that age was still around them and sometimes made its presence felt too easily within them. Thus their association together had to be kept pure and those who stepped too far out of line disciplined, even if necessary being expelled. They were a temporary community for their Lord would soon return and the world be wound up. If the future was brief the past was not. Paul grounded them firmly in Israel; Abraham was their father; the Old Testament was their book. They were no ephemeral group. They were God's group, his elect, who knew themselves to be his saints. They were the Body of that Christ who had redeemed them out of paganism. All the outside pressures on them also meant they were necessarily often thrown in on themselves. They emphasised their love for one another even as they were looking outwards to draw others into their company so that in the limited time remaining before the End more might be redeemed.

16

When Paul moved on from one of his newly founded churches to continue his mission he left behind him his own example, at least some stories of Jesus, though we are at a loss to know precisely which stories and how many and a holy book, the Greek translation of the Old Testament, the Septuagint. The way he uses the last in his letters shows it must have been known in some depth by at least some of his converts. Converted Jews would already know it; they probably brought actual copies along with them to the new Christian group. The educated would quickly learn to use these and teach others. Paul did not however normally leave behind him anyone in charge of the new congregation.[22] Leadership would have to develop within the group.[23]

What role was Paul to play in relation to a group after he had left it? Since people often play several roles simultaneously we should not be surprised to find Paul adopting a number towards his converts, and perhaps quite different roles towards those outside the community; with the latter we are not however concerned.

There are three basic types of role Paul might have adopted: one which set him on a superior plane to his converts, one which set him on the same level, and one which made him inferior. In the second type he and his converts would have (e.g. as brothers) a reciprocal role towards one another.

The best known model which Paul uses to relate the members of the groups to each other is that of the body, the church as the Body of Christ. In it the members exercise various functions for the benefit of the whole. We shall return to explore this more fully in Chapter VII. For the moment we look at the list of functions Paul associates with it in 1 Cor. 12.28-30 in order to enquire whether he saw himself as exercising any or all of them. We take them in reverse order. Paul tells us that he spoke in tongues (1 Cor. 14.18); this of course gave him no position of superiority in regard to the others since most of them in Corinth also did so (though some of them thought it gave them a position of superiority!).

It is by no means clear what is envisaged by 'helpers' (*antilēmpseis*) and 'administrators' (*kubernēseis*); Paul certainly exercised gifts of administration in managing the movements of his associates and in organizing the collection for Jerusalem. Some element of superiority would be involved. This would not however necessarily be true in relation to healing and the working of miracles. Acts tells us of this kind of activity on Paul's part and he refers to it in general terms in his letters (2 Cor. 12.12; cf. 1 Thess. 1.5) even if he records no specific events. But others also exercised these gifts.

The teacher can normally be regarded as superior to those he instructs at least in respect of what he teaches. Curiously Paul never explicitly terms himself a teacher but so much of his letters are taken up with teaching that we must classify him as such. However it is difficult to disentangle prophecy from teaching. If someone counsels others in the name of the Lord is he acting as prophet or teacher? Prophesy[24] can be either the foretelling of the future or the proclaiming of the truth of God in the present. The most detailed future prophecy Paul makes is in Acts 20.29,30 but the speech in which it is found may be a Lukan construction (see however also 1 Thess. 3.4; Gal. 5.21; 1 Cor. 15.51,52; Rom. 11.25,26 which might all be classified as future prophecies). On the other hand Paul consistently proclaims the truth of God in the present; in that sense he was a prophet, though he never so described himself. There is however indirect evidence to suggest that he regarded himself as one for he uses the words of Isaiah and Jeremiah to describe both his conversion and his later activity (Gal. 1.12,15,16; 1 Thess. 2.4; 2 Cor. 13.10).

If Paul was reticent in describing himself as a teacher and prophet he was not in calling himself an apostle.[25] This has led many to assume that the main role under which he viewed his relation to others was that of apostle and accordingly that his authority could be termed 'apostolic'. Yet when we examine the occasions when Paul speaks of himself as apostle it is never in the context of the exercise of authority.[26] We may approach his use of 'apostle' by asking when he first came to believe that he was an apostle. It is easy to answer that he was told this on the road to Damascus but this is highly unlikely since, if for no other reason, he would not have known at that time what the term meant. It is equally unlikely that when Ananias came to visit him that he hailed him as apostle. The first known instance of his use of the term is in 1 Thess. 2.6 and since he implies here that Silvanus and Timothy are also apostles he can hardly be using it in the way he later uses it when claiming to stand on equal terms with Peter. It is in this latter sense that he uses it in the addresses of his letters; yet it appears in only four, 1, 2 Corinthians and Galatians, in each of which he has to defend himself as being the equal of Peter or any of the other apostles, and in Romans. In the latter he is introducing himself to a church which did not know him and where he may suspect that critics have already attacked him and his message about the acceptance of Gentiles. He does not term himself an apostle in the addresses of 1 and 2 Thessalonians, Philippians and Philemon. When we examine how he uses it at later points in the letters we find it appearing in contexts where he is being compared unfavourably with the Jerusalem leaders (1 Cor. 9.1,2,5; 15.9; 2 Cor. 12.12). He also uses it frequently of the Jerusalem leaders or of others who have set themselves up as leaders (1 Cor. 15.7; 2 Cor. 11.5,13; 12.11; Gal. 1.17,19). If there are apostles then Paul affirms that he is one no less than Peter or anyone else who makes the claim. If any authority attaches to the term then Paul possesses it in no lesser degree than any other leader. Yet when we come in Chapter IV to look at how Paul exercises authority among his converts we shall discover that he never uses the term. He never reinforces what

19

he says by claiming to be an apostle. He has many ways of doing this but he never begins 'as an apostle I say to you...' or 'I instruct you as an apostle'.

The terms he uses most consistently to describe his relation with his converts derive from parenthood, terms curiously which do not appear in his lists of the gifts of the Spirit (Rom. 12.6-8; 1 Cor. 12.28-30). These terms[27] derive from the fact that it was his work which led his converts into Christianity. However we may briefly touch on another image which comes from his work as initial preacher, that of builder. He laid the foundations of the church on which others built (1 Cor. 3.10-15). Having first introduced the idea in that way he develops it. The Corinthians are his workmanship (1 Cor. 9.1). It is his aim to build up his converts in the faith, though should it be necessary he is also ready to tear down what he has already built (2 Cor. 10.8; 12.19; 13.10).[28]

Allied to the building imagery is the agricultural. Paul planted the church in Corinth, Apollos watered what Paul planted and God gave the increase (1 Cor. 3.6-9). Continued pastoral care is probably to be understood by the term 'watering' rather than that Paul converted the first believers and then Apollos came and converted more. That would entail an individualistic approach not normally found in Paul. Once the church has been founded there is pastoral work to be done as well as evangelism. Paul does his share of 'watering'. Before we leave this image let us note his explicit statement that growth comes from God. All Paul's pastoral work is done 'under God', and in the final issue is God's work and not Paul's. Paul may not always draw attention to this as he writes but in so far as in everything he does he believes he has the Spirit and is in Christ he is in fact asserting that his pastoral work is God's work. This comes out in the regular references he makes to his Lord, e.g. 'We beseech you and exhort you in the Lord Jesus ... you know what instructions we gave you through the

Lord Jesus'(1 Thess. 4.1,2). He can write in this way because he
believes that it was God who called and appointed him to his
work (Gal. 1.1,11- 17).

When he writes to the Romans Paul uses none of the images,
parenthood, planting, foundation-laying, which refer to the
beginning of his mission. They would have been inappropriate
since he had not founded the church in Rome. Thus when Paul
refers to his activity with these models he is consciously aware
both of their significance and of their limitations. His use is
deliberate, not haphazard.

In addition to those we have already mentioned Paul uses
several other images to relate himself to his churches. He terms
himself an ambassador at 2 Cor. 5.20 (and possibly also at
Philm 9[29]). We often take this as a term depicting Paul's role in
respect of his mission to the unconverted. He may have used it
in that way in sermons and letters we do not possess but in 2
Cor. 5.20 (and possibly Philm 9) it refers to his relation to his
converts. An ambassador carries the authority of his government and acts for it; so Paul carries the authority of Christ and
acts for him.

At 1 Cor. 4.1,2 Paul tells the Corinthians to regard him and
his associates 'as servants of Christ and stewards of the
mysteries of God.' At 9.17 he employs the verbal form of the
word 'steward' when he says that God has entrusted him with a
commission. In both cases Paul is describing his relation to
God and not to the Corinthians. A steward would normally
have some authority within a household and so as God's
steward Paul would have an authority in the church. The
nature of that authority is not clarified in his use of the image;
as we shall see in Chapter IV Paul has other ways of bringing
that out. We shall return to the image of 'slave' or 'servant' in
Chapter VII.[30]

There are a number of terms we might have expected Paul to
use of himself but of which there is no trace in his letters. In

Phil. 1.1 he mentions 'overseers' (*episkopoi*[31]). This term came rapidly to be used of one group of officers in the church, viz. bishops. Paul never uses it, nor more surprisingly the cognate verb, of himself and his work. Another word which he appears to use in a technical way of those occupying posts of responsibility in his churches is 'labour' (*kopiaō*). The Thessalonians are summoned to respect those who labour and are over them in the Lord (1 Thess. 5.12; cf 1 Cor. 16.16; Rom. 16.6,12). When however Paul uses the term of himself it is always in a general way (e.g. 1 Cor. 15.10; Phil. 2.16) and it tells us nothing of his relation to those among whom he labours.

A more striking omission is 'pastor' or 'shepherd' and associated words[32]. I had intended to call these lectures 'Paul the Pastor' until I discovered he never so described himself. It would probably have indicated their purpose more accurately than the present title. The image of the pastor was already in wide use. It is applied in the Old Testament both to God (Ps. 23; 77.20; Isa. 40.11; Jer. 31.10) and humans in respect of their relation to other humans (Num. 27.17; Jer. 3.15; 23.1-4; Ezek. 34; Zech. 11). Its use in this way was well known in the contemporary Middle East. It is regularly applied to, or used by, Jesus in the New Testament (Mark 6.34; 14.27; Luke 12.32; John 10.1-16; Heb. 13.20; 1 Pet. 2.25; Rev. 7.17). It is used of leaders in the church (Eph. 4.11; Acts 20.28,29; 1 Pet. 5.2,3; John 21.16; Rev. 2.27). It is impossible for us now to know why Paul avoided the term, perhaps because of its implications in relation to his converts—they were but poor silly sheep!

If Paul's speech to the elders of the church at Ephesus is genuine then Paul used the image, though not of himself but of the elders (the 'wolf' imagery is clearly associated with it).[33] Since the idea was widespread if Luke is summarising what Paul said he may have found it a useful word to describe the relation of leader to people, just as we use it to describe 1,2 Timothy, Titus though the word does not occur in them. For the same reason he may also have employed the term 'overseer' (v.28). We should however note the absence from the speech of the images Paul does use regularly of himself, e.g. parent, builder. This perhaps may confirm the view that we do not have here a verbatim account of what Paul said.

We normally think of a person to person relation in pastoral activity. Did Paul think of himself as counselling a number of individuals in the churches to which he wrote or as counselling groups? In the case of Philemon it must have been the former but in his other letters this is not so apparent. In them he rarely deals with individual cases. He addresses his letters to 'churches', and not even to groups of believers within churches. He envisages those to whom he writes as taking corporate action (1 Cor. 5.3-5; 2 Cor. 2.5-8). When in 2 Corinthians chapters 10-13 he writes strongly against those disturbing the church he nowhere appeals to a few faithful converts who might be expected to support him against the others. The individual members of the Body cannot act independently of other members; the Body must move as a whole.

His Converts View of Paul

It is not inappropriate to inquire what his converts thought of Paul as he fulfilled his various roles among them. We cannot draw any consistent picture for different churches will have had different opinions and these opinions will have changed from time to time. The Corinthians' initial enthusiasm for him has disappeared by 2 Corinthians chapters 10-13. We are moreover hindered in determining the views of his converts because we only possess his letters to them. He may have been ignorant of, withheld, or inadvertently misrepresented what they thought.

They would certainly have looked on him as the one who had first brought them the good news of salvation but if 1 Cor.

1.14-16 is anything to go by then most of them did not look on him as the one who had baptised them. Apparently he baptised one or two 'important' people at the beginning of each mission and then left it to them or others to baptise later converts. We do not know if when he was present he always insisted on presiding at the Eucharist. It is probable that the head of the home in which the service was held would normally preside, all the more so if an *agapē* was combined with the eucharist. Did Paul push aside that person when he was present? We have no knowledge whatsoever. All this suggests however that converts did not look on Paul as the one through whom the grace of the sacraments was ministered to them.

When Paul began work in a new city it was natural that the first converts should receive him enthusiastically. The Galatians, he says, received him as an angel and were ready to pluck out their eyes to help him (Gal. 4.14-15). The Thessalonians gave him a great welcome (1 Thess. 1.9). As long as he continued in good favour with his converts they would turn to him for help. The Corinthians wrote asking his advice on a number of matters which were puzzling them (1 Cor. 7.1), but times changed and portions of 2 Corinthians suggest that they considered him to be interfering in their affairs and attempting to control them when they were mature enough to look after themselves (see especially 2 Cor. 1.24). At one period they had a low opinion of his ability to present an effective argument (2 Cor. 11.6) and doubted his courage for his letters when he was away from them were tougher than his actual presence among them (2 Cor. 10.1,10). They also do not seem to have thought highly of him as a worker of miracles and a healer for he found it necessary to remind them of what he had done (2 Cor. 12.12). He may not have been thought a particularly spiritual man because he did not parade his gift of speaking in tongues (1 Cor. 14.18-19). He was accused of setting out to please people rather than to be firm and truthful (Gal. 1.10; cf. 1 Thess. 2.4). He was suspected of not being entirely honest in financial matters (2 Cor. 12.16). The Galatians came to look on him as an enemy because he told them the truth (Gal. 4.16).

On the other side of the coin they must have known something of his wonderful activity as a pioneer missionary and of what he suffered in that mission. It was often in their own communities that he had been attacked and ill-treated by pagan and Jewish opponents. Looking at him from yet another angle they would have seen him as the chief link between themselves and the other churches he had founded and probably also with that in Antioch. It was through him they heard of other Christians and what they were doing (2 Cor. 8.1-5) and through him that those other Christians learned of them (2 Cor. 9.1-2; 1 Thess. 1.8).[34]

This is a very mixed picture; Paul evoked a variety of reactions. Probably the reverence in which he is held today by the vast majority of Christians would never have crossed the minds of his original converts. Did they see him primarily as an authority figure or as their brother in Christ? As we go on we shall begin to get the glimour of an answer.

One final point: when we examine Paul's relations with his converts we should not expect surface consistency. They will have differed from one another, and we do not know all the ways in which they differed since we have no evidence other than his letters. Because they differed from one another what he may say to one church may seem inconsistent with what he says to another and because with the passage of time both he and they changed what he says in one letter to a church may seem inconsistent with what he says in another to the same church. Within any church there were different groupings and in a particular letter he may have one group in mind at one point and another at another. As time went by Paul himself may have grown in experience and so have abandoned earlier

25

methods and attitudes. Yet since he was active for a considerable period before his first letter and since pastors form their
main attitudes and methods during their first years of pastoral
work it would be surprising to find great variations in Paul with
the passage of time.

NOTES

1. It is possible that Romans chap 16 was not written to Rome but to
another church of Paul's foundation. This is uncertain and there is little in
the chapter which would in any case assist our inquiry.

2. It is unnecessary for our purposes to discuss whether letters like
Philippians are amalgams of a number of Pauline letters since all the
material is Pauline and written to converts.

3. See Best, *A Commentary on The First and Second Epistles to the
Thessalonians*, A.& C. Black, London, 1972, pp. 50-58.

4. See e.g. R.P. Martin, *Colossians and Philemon* (New Century Bible),
Eerdmans, Grand Rapids and Marshall, London, 1978, ad v.19.

5. D. Guthrie, *New Testament Introduction*, Tyndale, London (3rd edn),
p.637.

6. See pp. 21, 52, 68, 97f, 150f

7. In addition to the commentaries see J. Lambrecht, 'Paul's Farewell-
Address at Miletus (Acts 20.17-38)' in *Les Actes des Apôtres* (BETL
XLVIII) Duculot, Gembloux and Leuven University Press, 1979, pp.
307-337, and C.K. Barrett 'Paul's Address to the Ephesian Elders' in
God's Christ and His People (Studies in Honour of Nils Alstrup Dahl, ed.
J.Jervell and W.A.Meeks), Universitetsforlaget, Oslo,1977, pp.107-121.

8. See pp. 145f

9. See pp. 22f

10. See pp. 18, 22f, 72n.19, 94n.6, 116, 145f

11. See chapter V.

12. See Best, 'A Damascus Road Experience?', *Irish Biblical Studies*, 7
(1985), pp.2-7.

13. Cf. F.F.Bruce, *I & II Corinthians* (New Century Bible), Eerdmans,
Grand Rapids and Marshall, London, 1980, p.142.

14. See Best, 'The Revelation to Evangelize the Gentiles', *J.T.S.* 35 (1984),
pp. 1-30.

15. This is strongly argued by A.T. Hanson, *The Pioneer Ministry*,
S.C.M., London, 1961, pp. 61-2.

16. E.g. see G. Theissen, *The Social Setting of Pauline Christianity* (E.T.
by J.H. Schütz), T. & T. Clark, Edinburgh, 1982, pp. 69-119; Wayne A.

Meeks, *The First Urban Christians*, Yale University Press, New Haven and London, 1983, pp. 51-73.

17. This is suggested by D. Patte, *Paul's Faith and the Power of the Gospel*, Fortress, Philadelphia, 1983, p.36.

18. While Acts and Colossians are not by Paul there is no reason to suppose they do not give us a reliable picture of the constituency from which converts were drawn.

19. See Robert Banks, *Paul's Idea of Community*, Paternoster, Exeter, 1980, p. 38.

20. See the calculation in J. Murphy-O'Connor, *St. Paul's Corinth: Texts and Archeology*, (Good News Studies 6), Michael Glazier, Wilmington, Delaware, 1983 p. 156.

21. Murphy-O'Connor, op. cit., p.159.

22. Cf Roland Allen, *Missionary Methods: St. Paul's or Ours*, Robert Scott, London, 1912, pp. 113-4. Allen (p. 116) instances Philippi as a possible exception since in Acts 16.11-16 where Paul arrives at that city we have a 'we-passage' and at 20.6 when he returns the beginning of another which suggests Luke may have been there all the time. This would have been a very lengthy period. Paul stayed a few months in Thessalonica, at least eighteen in Corinth (Acts 18.11), and two years in Ephesus. To this we must add time spent in travelling to Caesarea and Antioch. There is no reason to suppose the author of Acts spent all this time in Philippi.

23. On leadership see below pp. 86f, 144f

24. On Paul as prophet see e.g. J. Murphy-O'Connor, *Paul on Preaching*, Sheed & Ward, London and New York, 1964, pp.104-145; J.M. Myers and J.D. Freed, 'Is Paul Also Among the Prophets', *Interpretation*, 20 (1966), pp. 40-53; David Hill, *New Testament Prophecy*, Marshall, London, 1979, pp. 111-140.

25. On 'apostle' see e.g. C.K. Barrett, *The Signs of an Apostle*, Epworth, London, 1970; W. Schmithals, *The Office of Apostle in the Early Church*, Abingdon, Nashville, 1969.

26. See Best, 'Paul's Apostolic Authority—?' *J.S.N.T.* 27 (1986), pp. 3-25.

27. See chapter II.

28. See below pp. 39f, 87-90

29. Many manuscripts read here *presbutēs* ='old man' rather than *presbeutēs* = 'ambassador' and it is perhaps the better reading.

30. See pp. 135, 149

31. This word is sometimes translated 'bishop' but the title had not been formalised at this stage and so the neutral rendering 'overseer' is preferable.

32. In 1 Cor. 9.7 Paul is no more likening himself to a shepherd than he is to a soldier.

33. See above pp. 5f

34. Cf. B. Holmberg, *Paul and Power: The Structure of Authority in the Primitive Church as Reflected in the Pauline Epistles*, Gleerup, Lund, 1978, pp. 74-5.

II

FATHERLY CARE[1]

Paul's love for his converts

As we have seen there are two basic types of model used by Paul to portray his relationship to his converts, the reciprocal and the superior/inferior. We shall now concentrate on the latter and return to the former in Chapter VII. A superior/inferior relation might suggest an authoritarian relation but it need not if its governing power is love. Whichever model controls Paul he always believes that he acts out of love for his converts.

In his earliest extant letter he writes, 'So being affectionately desirous of you, we were ready to share with you not only the gospel of God but also our own selves, because you had become very dear to us' (1 Thess. 2.8). Indeed wherever we open his letters they are full of expressions of love for their recipients (cf. 2 Cor. 2.4; 5.14; 6.11-13; 7.3; Phil. 1.7; 4.1; 1 Thess. 2.7, 17). The word love itself may not be used but we sense the feeling in the intensity of his prayers (e.g. Phil. 1.4,9; 1 Thess. 3.10). It may be easy to love and pray for far-off anonymous groups. Paul knows the groups to which he writes and he regularly stresses his concern for them as individuals with phrases like 'you all' (1 Thess. 1.2).

He often calls his converts 'his beloved' (1 Cor. 4.14; 15.58; Phil. 2.12; Philm 16). It is not the term of endearment which comes readily to a pastor's lips in our western culture but in some cultures it is an accepted way of addressing those one loves. Paul's use of the names of his recipients often softens what may otherwise seem a harsh statement, e.g. 'O foolish Galatians' (Gal. 3.1; cf. 2 Cor. 6.11; Phil. 4.15).

Had he not loved his converts Paul need never have written to them after he had left them. While it is true that some of his letters, or parts of them, are very much given over to defending himself all of them at least in part deal with the actual situation of his converts. He had been alarmed by reports from Chloe's people about the situation in Corinth and had also received a letter from the Corinthians themselves seeking his advice (1 Cor. 1.11; 7.1). He did not need to reply to their questions or comment on the reports. He could have shrugged them off or detailed one of his assistants to go to Corinth and sort out the issues while he himself got on with earning his living and evangelising elsewhere. Instead he wrote at length. In the long list of his trials in 2 Cor. 11.22-29 the final and climactic item is 'the daily pressure upon me of my anxiety for all the churches.'

His concern emerges in other ways. At one point he sent Titus to Corinth to straighten out problems that had arisen after 1 Corinthians was written. In the meantime he commenced mission work in Troas. He was however so anxious to learn how Titus had got on that he could not settle down to preaching but dashed off across to Europe to meet Titus as soon as possible and learn his news (2 Cor. 2.12-13). On another occasion when no news arrived about what was happening in Thessalonica and he was not himself able to return he sent Timothy to establish the converts in their faith and to counsel them lest their afflictions should disturb them (1 Thess. 3.1-3). In more general terms he writes 'Who is weak, and I am not weak? Who is made to fall, and I am not indignant?' (2 Cor. 11.29). 1 Cor. 9.19-22 has been interpreted in many ways, from a cynical disregard for principles to deep concern. The passage falls in the middle of a discussion about eating food which had been sacrificed to idols. Within that context it indicates Paul's willingness to adapt himself to the situation of his readers. If he is ready to behave as a Jew to win Jews and as a Gentile to win Gentiles he will be ready to accomodate himself to the ideas of his converts on food. His love for his converts will make him ever adaptable to their needs. He himself did not believe in any deity other than his own. Meat was not contaminated in any way by being sacrificed to a pagan god. But if he was living with some of his converts who had not thought through the matter as he had, what should he do? He says he will voluntarily abstain, 'If food is a cause of my brother's falling, I will never eat meat, lest I cause my brother to fall' (1 Cor. 8.13). His refusal is an expression of his love.

In 1 Thess. 2.9 he tells his converts that while he was with them he worked day and night that he 'might not burden any of' them while he evangelised the city. Though accepting money from them would have made things easier for him he refused it because he loved them. In one remarkable passage (2 Cor. 11.17) where he is defending himself against false accusations he says that he has been forced to boast though this boasting has not been done with the Lord's authority. He acknowledges that what he does is wrong in God's eyes yet he goes on to do it so that he may deliver his converts from those who preach a false gospel. He is prepared to go against God's will for the sake of his converts. This is indeed love and on a par with Rom. 9.3 where he affirms his readiness to go to hell if only his fellow Jews would acknowledge Jesus as their Messiah.

The area where we normally expect to see love most clearly and effectively in action is the family. It is not then surprising that Paul uses family images to display his concern for his converts. He depicts himself as their brother, father, mother and them as his brothers and children. For the moment we leave aside the 'brotherly' model (see Chapter VII) and turn to the parental.

Contemporary Parenthood[2]
That Paul should cast himself more regularly in the role of

'father' rather than 'mother' is not surprising since he lived in a patriarchal society. W.K. Lacey writes:

> Greek society was (and is) patriarchal: the master of the *oikos* was the head of the family, its *kyrios*, as its governor, governing the slaves as master, the children as a sort of king because of their affection for him and his greater age, his wife like a political leader, differing from normal political leadership only in that this relationship does not involve change of leaders, as self-governing states normally change their leaders, but the husband is always head of the family.[3]

The position of a father was more clearly defined under Roman law than in Greece; the paterfamilias[4]

> was the domestic magistrate ... with absolute authority in his own house, whither the public authority did not penetrate.

His judgements could include 'the penalties of exclusion from the *domus*, imprisonment, scourging or death'.[5] In the Empire the father's authority was beginning to wane but still existed in our period.

In Rome the father's power ended only with his death; in Greece when he was about sixty he usually handed over authority to his eldest married son (males married around the age of thirty)[6]. Women of course did have a role in the family but it normally related only to the younger children and we may note that Paul's two clear references to himself as mother of his converts (Gal. 4.19; 1 Thess. 2.7) relate to their conversion and early period as Christians.

Paul's converts came from a society governed by Greek and Roman ideas (Corinth though in Greece was a Roman city); he himself came from Jewish society, even though one much affected by Hellenism in Tarsus. He will therefore have gathered many of his ideas of the family from Judaism. In an intimate matter like family life we are ruled largely by what happens in our early years. Paul will also have been a close observer of non- Jewish society. Yet even if the ideas which controlled him came from Judaism they would not have differed greatly from those that would have influenced him if he had been born a Gentile. If there had been much difference his converts would probably not have been as prepared as they were to accept him as their parent.

The Jewish child was expected to honour his parents and in particular his father. Beginning at least with the Ten Commandments this stress which of course is also found in Hellenism appears in every period of Judaism.[7] From literature close to Paul's day we pick Sir. 3.1-9

> Whoever honours his father atones for sins
> and whoever glorifies his mother is like one who lays up treasure ...
> Honour your father by word and deed, that a blessing from him may come upon you.

Philo could even write

> Some bolder spirits, glorifying the name of parenthood, say that a father and mother are in fact gods revealed to sight who copy the Uncreated in His work as the Framer of life.[8]

In later rabbinic Judaism many sermons were deliverd on this theme, and delivered to adult children.[9] Since honouring parents includes obedience to them failure to show respect implies disobedience and is subject to discipline: 'He who spares the rod hates his son, but he who loves him is diligent to discipline him' (Prov. 13.24)[10]. Such obedience to parents is also stressed in the Christian *Haustafeln* (Eph. 6.1; Col. 3.20).

In Judaism as in the Greek and Roman worlds the father was responsible for the instruction of his children.[11] Thus in Deut. 6.7 the father is told to teach his children 'Hear, O Israel: the Lord our God is one Lord; and you shall love the Lord your God with all your heart, and with all your soul, and with all your might'. So also the writer of Proverbs says

When I was a son with my father, tender, the only one in the sight of my mother, he taught me, and said to me, 'Let your heart hold fast my words; keep my commandments and live' (4.3-4).

The mother was not excluded from teaching (Prov. 6.20) but her instruction would be directed towards the younger children.

The Metaphor of Parenthood

Since Paul was not the biological parent of his converts we need to look briefly at the way the contemporary world used the metaphor of parenthood. In the Wisdom literature the sage describes those he instructs as his sons (used widely in Proverbs, e.g. 3.1; 4.1, and occasionally in Sirach, 7.3; 39.13). This usage continued well beyond the New Testament period and is found in *The Teaching of Silvanus*, one of the wisdom writings from Nag Hammadi (VII 4). The author of the Qumran Hymns says 'Thou hast made me a father to the sons of grace' (1QH 7.20b-22) and the 'overseer' is to love the members of the community 'as a father loves his children' (CD 13.9).[13] Some rabbinic sayings though they come from a slightly later period suggest that the idea was a commonplace in the instruction of the rabbis: 'He who teaches the son of his neighbour the Torah, Scripture ascribes it to him as if he begotten him' (b Sanh. 19b).[14] Even within the New Testament Paul was not the only one to use the idea. The author of 1 John repeatedly addresses his readers as 'children' (2.1,12,18,28).

If the metaphor was one which would have come naturally to Paul from his Jewish background it is not one which would have been foreign to his Gentile converts. Rulers thought of themselves as fathers of their peoples (Dio Chrys. *Or* 1.22-23). Cities which founded colonies were regularly known as 'mother-cities' (*metropoleis*).[16] The Athenians therefore term themselves 'fathers' of the Ionians (Herod. 7.51; 8.22; Plut. *Them.* 9). Romulus was known as the 'father' of Rome (Liv.

1.16.3; 5.49.7). Philo terms Jerusalem the mother city not only of Judaea but also of the diaspora (*Leg. ad Gaium* 281). When we move away from the political sphere we still find the metaphor in use. Epictetus tells us that the Cynic philosopher 'has made all mankind his children; the men among them he has as his sons, the women as daughters' (iii.22,81)[17]. In Apuleius' fable *The Golden Ass* once Lucius has been changed back from the form of an ass into his proper human form through the mysteries of Isis he calls the officiating priest, Mithras, his spiritual father (XI 25.7; cf. 21.3) In Tractate XIII of the Corpus Hermeticum, which deals with rebirth, Hermes as father communicates an understanding of rebirth to Tat as son (13.1,2).[18] The metaphor of course can be linked relatively easily to the concept of rebirth.

Paul's use of the metaphor[19]

It is impossible and for our purposes unnecessary to determine from where Paul derived the image in relation to himself. If he derived it from the Wisdom Literature he will of course have appreciated its appropriateness for his non-Jewish converts because of its Hellenistic usage. He views himself as parent of his converts from the moment of their conversion and because of his association with their conversion (1 Cor. 4.15; Gal. 4.19). Other images confirm Paul's belief that he had a special connection with the beginning of the Christian life of his converts: he is the master builder who laid the foundations; he planted his churches, others tend them as they grow (1 Cor. 3.10,6). The initiatory parental role comes out again in 2 Cor. 12.14 where, explaining his unwillingness to accept financial support from the Corinthians, he bases this on his parenthood. The slave Onesimus became his child when he was converted (Philm 10).

Paul's parental love towards his converts is seen when as he returns Onesimus to Philemon he refers to him as his 'very heart'(v.12). It appears in 1 Thess. 2.7 in the very use of the word gentle if 'gentle' ēpioi is read here rather than 'babes' nēpioi.[20] In 1 Cor. 4.14 Paul calls the Corinthians his 'beloved' children and this though they have been showing themselves very troublsesome children. As a good parent Paul answers his childrens' questions but he does much more than give advice and information; he seeks to deal with their underlying fears and anxieties. The Thessalonians had asked him about the timing of the parousia and as he answers them at the same time he attempts to set their hearts and minds at rest in 5.1-11. 1 Cor. 7.32 shows him keen that his converts should be free from worry; the hymn of love (1 Corinthians chapter 13) is set in the midst of worries about charismata.

In his role as parent it is natural that he should exhort and encourage his children (1 Thess. 2.11; cf 1 Cor. 4.14). In 2 Cor. 6.13 he addresses his readers as children as he instructs them and as Furnish comments he 'lapses momentarily into the use of the first person singular (6.13), in order to emphasise that he is calling upon them as his spiritual *children*.'[21]

Paul switches at times in an interesting way between the male and female forms of the parental image.[22] He implies to the Galatians that he is their mother because he endured birth pangs at their conversion (Gal. 4.19). He tells the Thessalonians that he is their nurse; this again suggests the role of mother since in those days most children were nursed by their mothers (1 Thess. 2.7). This use of the image may well come from Cynic circles.[23] The female image is also present in 1 Cor. 3.1-3 where Paul speaks of feeding his converts with milk; while fathers today may bottle-feed their babies in the ancient world babies were breast fed. There are a couple of instances where it is difficult to decide whether Paul has the male or the female image in view. At both 1 Cor. 4.15 and Philm 10 he speaks of 'begetting' (*gennao*) children. While this verb is normally used of fathers it is also used of the mother's bearing of the child;

36

because the word 'father' also appears in 1 Cor. 4.15 it must have the male meaning there; either is possible in Philm 10.[24]

The earliest evidence for Paul's use of the parental role is found in 1 Thess. 2.7,11; here it appears in both male and female forms. The context is Paul's claim to sincerity. In the contemporary world there were many travelling teachers, philosophers and preachers who depended for their livelihood on the fees paid by their hearers. Among them were quacks who were more concerned with the fees than the truth of what they taught. Paul apparently had been accused of behaving like these quacks. He defends himself: 'We never used either words of flattery, as you know, or a cloak of greed, as God is witness; nor did we seek glory from men, whether from you or from others,' and continues 'But we were gentle [25] among you, like a nurse taking care of her children' (1 Thess. 2.5-7). Parents are sincere with their own children whatever they are to those of others. So Paul goes on 'You are witnesses, and God also, how holy and righteous and blameless was our behaviour to you believers; for you know, how like a father with his children, we exhorted each one of you and encouraged you and charged you' (2.10-11).

In the ancient world as we have seen the father bore a special role in relation to the education of his children and it is very difficult to separate the teaching and fatherly roles in Paul. Presumably he himself would never have done so. While today we still recognize how important it is for parents to instruct their children education has become so specialised that it is impossible for most parents to be responsible for much more than the moral element in the upbringing of their children. Paul as parent of his converts supplies them with the deeper knowledge of their Christian faith as well as answering their requests for information about marriage and the timing of the parousia.

In his teaching Paul like any parent is fearlessly honest:

There is no attempt to keep the door open by partial statements, no concealment of the real issue and all that is involved, no timid fear of giving offence, no suggestion of possible compromise, no attempt to make things really difficult appear easy.[26]

Such sincerity often means that the one who exercises it must hurt in order to help. Faced with a difficult situation in Corinth Paul wrote the church a very strong and plain letter. After its despatch he worried about its effect, as many of us do with our letters. So he waited anxiously for news of its reception and when he learned of its successful outcome he wrote again to the church

For even if I made you sorry with my letter, I do not regret it (though I did regret it), for I see that that my letter grieved you, though only for a while. As it is. I rejoice, not because you were grieved, but because you were grieved into repenting; for you felt a godly grief, so that you suffered no loss through us (2 Cor. 7.8,9).

Parents and teachers must always be able to speak freely to their children. When Paul had spoken strongly to the Galatians he asked them 'Have I then become your enemy by telling you the truth'? (4.16). Equally parents and teachers expect that their children will speak openly to them. So Paul says to the Corinthians 'Our mouth is open to you, Corinthians; our heart is wide ...In return—I speak as to children—widen your hearts also... Open your hearts to us' (2 Cor. 6.11,13; 7.2).

If Paul calls his converts his children what are we to think when he calls them sons (and daughters) of God? Can both God and Paul be fathers of the same believers? The possibilities of confusion are removed once we realise that Paul derived these two aspects of the one metaphor from different metaphorical fields. Paul invented neither metaphorical field and when he brought them together he did not see any reason to unify them; he may not even have been aware that he was using the same term in two different metaphorical senses. It is something we all do. The metaphor of Paul as parent with which we are principally concerned was picked up from the ancient world in general where it was widespread. The metaphor of God as Father came to Paul almost exclusively from Judaism, the teaching of Jesus and primitive Christianity. The impact of this usage is seen in the retention within the church of the Aramaic word *abba* for God as Father (Rom. 8.15; Gal. 4.6).[27]

Maturity

Good parents (or teachers) view their primary task as that of enabling their children to grow up, to mature, to become adults. Some day the children will have to live on their own and make their own decisions. It is therefore proper to inquire if Paul enables his converts to mature and grow in the faith. Success here would obviously require great tact on his part. For, though his converts were babes in the faith, they were grown men and women who were used to taking decisions for themselves; they would not take kindly to being treated as infants. Paul had been a Christian for many years before he came to any of the churches to which he wrote his letters and he had had time to mature in the faith. Yet even if he had been a Christian only a few months he still had a much more mature position as a Jew from which to begin than had his Gentile converts. Exclusive claims in matters of belief were not new to Paul. As a Jew he had already thought about how to deal with food sacrificed to idols and though as a Christian he could bring new light to this and other problems he was on the way to having his mind made up before he was converted.

Maturity and growth link themselves directly to some of the other models Paul uses to depict his work. This is particularly so when be pictures himself as a builder.[28] Paul and others (e.g. Apollos) are engaged in building up the Corinthian Christians and so he says 'Let each ... take care how he builds' (1 Cor.

3.10), and does not exclude himself from his warning. Growth is also the underlying idea where Paul plants and Apollos waters, God giving the increase (1 Cor. 3.6).

In the discussion over food sacrificed to idols some believers found it almost impossible to eat such food because of its association with their past pagan lives. Others had no difficulty and apparently flaunted their moral strength before those who were in doubt. Paul is forced to remind them of the difficulties of the weak and says to them ' "All things are lawful" (probably he is quoting here something they themselves have said) but not all things build up' (1 Cor. 10.23). Christians ought to be building up one another in the faith (1 Thess. 5.11). Practically the same argument appears in relation to charismatic gifts. The true test of their use is their ability to assist others to mature: 'since you are eager for manifestations of the Spirit, strive to excel in building up the church' (1 Cor. 14.12). Maturity is again the theme in v.20. The Corinthians ought then to behave like adults, indeed like Paul himself. There is a time to pass from childhood to adulthood (1 Cor. 13.11). Paul prays for the Philippians that they may grow in love and moral discernment (Phil. 1.9-10). He even addresses them as already mature: 'Let those of us who are mature be thus minded; and if in anything you are otherwise minded, God will reveal that also to you' (3.15).

Paul assumes some measure of maturity on the part of his converts whenever he writes to them, as he often does, 'Do you not know': 'Do you not know that you are God's temple and that God's Spirit dwells in you?' (1 Cor. 3.16; cf. 5.6; 6.2, 15; 9.24). In saying this he implies that they have been Christian long enough for this knowledge to have become part of their life and for them to realise their own maturity without him constantly reminding them. There is indeed no need for him to remind them for God himself has taught them the supreme lesson of loving one another (1 Thess. 4.9). His converts have been Christian long enough for them to be able to make their own decisions. This is especially so in relation to the Eucharist where he says he speaks 'as to sensible men; judge for yourselves what I say' (1 Cor. 10.15) and bids them look into themselves when they come to the meal: 'Let a man examine himself, and so eat of the bread and drink of the cup' (1 Cor. 11.28). Later to those same converts when things have gone badly wrong and they are in danger of rejecting him he says 'Examine yourselves, to see whether you are holding to your faith' (2 Cor. 13.5).

Paul gave his converts freedom to make their own decisions in many matters. Though he could have commanded Philemon to send Onesimus back to him so that he, Paul, could use him, he appeals to him instead for love's sake (vv.8-9). He does not conceal from the Thessalonians the sufferings that lie ahead of them (1 Thess. 1.6; 2.2,14; 3.3). He hopes that the church in Corinth will be suffcently mature to contain within itself those converts who have been going to law with one another; they are not just fresh converts and should be able to settle among themselves whatever quarrels arise (1 Cor. 6.1-7). In relation to marriage Paul has his own view of the superiority of celibacy but he does not force this on his converts; he leaves them to make up their own minds (1 Cor. 7.25-35). The same personal and individual decision is left to the man with the 'betrothed' (the precise determination of the meaning of this word does not affect the issue); he must decide for himself (1 Cor. 7.36-8).

Most new organisations when they first come into existence are quick to devise ways of administering themselves; Paul does not lay down a form of organisation for his churches but leaves them free to develop as they wish. Bishops and deacons appear at Philippi (Phil. 1.1) but not in the other Pauline churches. In Thessalonica the leaders do not have any particular title; they are just those who 'labour among you and are over you in the Lord' (1 Thess. 5.12). Leaders as such are not mentioned as present in Corinth; there is a vague reference to being subject to Stephanas and such fellow workers (1 Cor. 16.15-16). Those referred to in the list of 12.28-30 are never addressed in the letter; the terms describing them are functional rather than indicative of position or status. At Gal. 6.6 an imprecise group of teachers appears. Paul's churches were then free to develop under the Spirit.[29] If he did not impose a precise system of government on them neither did he impose a rigid creed. We find him employing not one but a number of early confessions and the like (e.g. 1 Cor. 15.3-5; 1 Thess. 1.9-10; Rom. 1.3-4; Phil. 2.6-11). Since he himself baptised only a few (1 Cor. 1.14-17) he probably left the decision as to who should be baptised to those who administered the sacrament or to the decision of the church as a whole.[30]

In other and wider ways Paul shows that he regards his converts as at least partially mature. It is implicit every time he uses a rational argument to persuade them to carry out some duty or to accept some teaching. The argument may not always appear reasonable to us because we may not accept all of its premises as when he advises celibacy on account of the nearness of the end (1 Cor. 7.29, 31). Equally we may not accept the type of argument he uses when he allegorises the story of Sarah and Hagar (Gal. 4.21-31). However what is significant is not our view of the validity of such arguments but that Paul reasons with his converts and does not simply impose duties or beliefs on them. Children regularly complain that adults just tell them what to do and believe and never explain. When Paul explains he treats his converts as grown-up. So when he works his way through the complicated discusssion on whether to eat food sacrificed to idols or not he leaves the final decision to the individual: 'I speak as to sensible men; judge for yourselves what I say' (1 Cor. 10.15). Even if they reject Paul's advice there is no suggestion that they be excluded from the church or disciplined in any way. Paul hopes his approach to his converts is always one of reason; he never comes to them with 'plausible words of wisdom' (1 Cor. 2.4), that is to say he does not attempt to persuade them with passionate rhetoric or light-fingered logic. He treats them as mature people who can make mature judgements.

Freedom is related to maturity. It is the ideal for the Christian (Gal. 5.1, 'For freedom Christ has set us free') and can be exercised only by the mature adult. Yet few are genuinely mature. So freedom needs to be controlled and Gal. 5.1 leads on to Gal. 5.13, 'do not use your freedom as an opportunity for the flesh'. If freedom is to be controlled it must be by love, love for others (5.14). Paul does not however always find this love within his congregations; they 'bite and devour' one another (5.15). This failure leads us on to our next section, for though Paul regularly treats his converts as mature he is well aware that they are not always such.

Lack of maturity

There are few parents who would not agree that while they aim to let their children grow to maturity there are times when that maturity seems far off and it is difficult to treat them as mature. So there are times when Paul realises that his converts are not as mature as he would like them to be. He complains that he has not been able to teach the Corinthians as he wished for he 'could not address' them 'as spiritual men, but [only] as men of the flesh, as babes in Christ' who were not ready for adult food (1 Cor. 3.1,2). While he expects those same Corinthians to contain their quarrels within their community their imma-turity is seen in that this has not happened: there is no one among them 'wise enough to decide between members of the brotherhood' (1 Cor. 6.5).

Paul is aware that there is much he has yet to give his converts before they can in all honesty be viewed as mature. He would love to visit them to supply what is lacking in their faith. Yet if he cannot visit he can at least pray for their growth (1 Thess. 3.11-13; cf. Phil. 1.9-11). They are on the way but more is required, more indeed of what they are already supplying in their love: they love all the brethren 'but we exhort you, brethren, to do so more and more' (1 Thess. 4.10; cf. 4.1).

This recognition on Paul's part that his converts are not as mature as he would like and his desire that they continue to grow is what we would expect from any good parent. Some of the ways however in which he seeks to encourage their growth may not be the kind of which we would approve in a good parent.

A parent may say to a child: 'Don't do that; if you do I'll look a fool in the eyes of people!' The child is expected to behave in a certain way not for its own good but for the parent's benefit. This does not help the child to mature. Paul comes dangerously close to this type of argument when he appeals to the Corinthians to forsake immoral behaviour; he fears that 'when I come again my God may humble me before you' (2 Cor. 12.21). He enourages the Philippians to persevere 'so that in the day of Christ I may be proud that I did not run in vain or labour in vain' (2.16; cf. Gal. 4.11; 1 Thess. 2.19). In his attempt to persuade the Corinthians to contribute more to the collection for Jerusalem he at times leaves the impression that he is as worried about his own reputation as he is about the poor in Jerusalem or the unity of Jew and Gentile in the one church. Having boasted earlier to other churches about the Corinthian generosity he is now afraid that if they are not generous his boast will be shown up and he be humiliated (2 Cor. 9.3,4).

Parents have been known to remind their children how much they have given up for them in their attempt to persuade them to do what they, their parents, wish. Their interest is focussed on themselves and they fail to treat their children as mature. Paul can fail in this way. When he sends Onesimus back to Philemon he assures the latter that he will repay whatever is necessary, but goes on to take away from his generosity by adding 'to say nothing of your owing me even your own self' (v.19). Philemon would not be a Christian but for Paul (cf. Gal. 6.17).[31] Children as they grow up increasingly dislike the parental approach which begins: 'Do as I say; I am your parent'. In effect this is Paul's approach in 1 Cor. 4.15 when he writes 'For though you have countless guides in Christ, you do not have many fathers' (cf. Gal. 5.9,10). His converts ought to live in ways that will please their spiritual father (Phil. 2.2,16).

Parents do not help their children to grow when they make them feel ashamed if they fail to carry out their parents' wishes. In the matter of the collection Paul holds up the example of the Macedonians to the Corinthians with the implication that they will feel ashamed if they fall below that example (2 Cor. 8.1-7). When the Corinthians are in danger of behaving immorally because they do not take the resurrection sufficently seriously he says to them 'Come to your right mind, and sin no more. For some have no knowledge of God. I say this to your shame' (1 Cor. 15.34; cf. 6.5; 2 Cor. 11.7-11; in 1 Cor. 4.14 he rejects this approach).

In all of this it is not simply a question whether Paul employs wrong methods of persuasion but whether he treats his converts in ways that help them to mature. Rightly or wrongly we often stimulate rivalry between children in the hope that they will benefit from it. Paul did this in respect of the collection. He holds before both Corinthians and Macedonians the example of the other and praises it trusting that thereby both will give more (2 Cor. 8.1-7; 9.1-5). He can be excused in doing this if his main objective is the relief of poverty in Jerusalem or the preservation of the unity of the church which is in danger of splitting into Jewish and Gentile sections. He cannot be excused if his only intention was to save himself embarrassment when one or other church failed to provide what he had boasted it would provide. Probably it is impossible to isolate here just one motive as governing Paul's conduct.

The same kind of difficulty exists when Paul uses flattery to advance either his own ends or the good of his converts. The former is clearly much more reprehensible than the latter. Although Paul denied that he ever used 'words of flattery' (1 Thess. 2.5) there are obvious instances where he does. He tells the Corinthians that they 'excel in everything' (2 Cor. 8.7) so as to persuade them to contribute more to the collection for Jerusalem. When he tells the Thessalonians that they are his 'glory and joy' (1 Thess. 2.20) it is within the context of his concern for them. When at the beginning of his letters he speaks apparently flatteringly of those to whom he writes he is not out of line with comtemporary practice.[32] This 'flattery' appears regularly in the Pauline corpus[33] and is no worse than when we commence a letter 'Dear...'to someone we do not regard as 'dear' at all. Among the genuine Pauline letters this approach is found in Philemon and 1 and 2 Thessalonians, which are not polemical letters where there is no reason then to cajole his readers. Paul's letters moreover are neither private letters nor letters for publication; they are intended to be read aloud in the churches to which they are sent. In that respect they are more like speeches and it is customary to commence speeches with a 'flattering' reference (the *captatio benevolentiae*) to their hearers (cf Acts 24.2,3; 26.2,3). When Paul describes his readers as saints or sons of light (1 Thess. 5.5-6) this is not flattery because it is true as a statement about their position before God.[34] In none of these cases does he gain any personal advantage through his flattery. This however is no longer so when he says to the Corinthians 'I have great confidence in you; I have great pride in you' (2 Cor. 7.4) and does so in a context in which his own prestige is at stake; such passages are however few in number.

If Paul's behaviour occasionally then falls short of what we might expect we need to note that he can criticise his own supporters as easily as he flatters them. He approves as little of a Pauline party in Corinth as he does of a Petrine (1 Cor. 1.11-17). Later in writing to the same church when his position has come under severe attack he is to be found opposing contentiousness as such and not just that of those who oppose him (2 Cor. 12.20-13.4). His supporters come under equal rebuke with his opponents.

Children are often threatened with what will happen to them if they do wrong or promised rewards if they are good. If we leave aside all consideration of the morality of such an approach we are still faced with the question whether this is a good way of helping children to mature. Occasionally Paul threatens his readers by reminding them of God's judgement. The work of each in building up the community will be judged and indifferent work burnt up, though the one at fault may be saved (1 Cor. 3.10-15). All should make it their aim to please God for 'we must all appear before the judgement seat of Christ, so that each one may receive good or evil, according to what he has done in the body' (2 Cor. 5.9-10; cf 1 Cor. 11.29-30; 1 Thess. 4.6). In these cases he carefully includes himself among those whom God will judge and adopts no superior attitude; when God judges he himself may turn out to be as guilty as any of his converts. This qualification however disappears when he presents himself as the instrument of God's punishment. He asks the Corinthians 'Shall I come to you with a rod, or with love in a spirit of gentleness?' (1 Cor. 4.21; cf. 2 Cor. 13.1-2). Here the threatened punishment probably belongs to this world.

As well as threatening Paul promises rewards. These may belong to this world as in his promise to the Corinthians that if they give generously to the collection they will 'have enough of everything' (2 Cor. 9.8; cf. v.6). He also promises rewards in the next world. In the passage just quoted he goes on to assure his readers that God will increase the harvest of their righteousness and that they will glorify God by their obedience (2 Cor.9.10,13). All this will come to fruition on the day of judgement.

If it is doubtful whether the promise of reward and the threat of punishment lead to genuine maturity the same is true of that use of sarcasm with which Paul sometimes attacks his converts. The Corinthians, or more probably some of them, have apparently believed that they have already attained their final position in God's kingdom and Paul mocks them 'Already you have become rich! Without us you have become kings! ... We are fools for Christ's sake, but you are wise in Christ. We are weak, but you are strong. You are held in honour, but we in disrepute' (1 Cor. 4.8,10). When he ends his defence of his rejection of financial maintenance from the Corinthians he cries 'Forgive me this wrong!' (2 Cor. 12.13). Other instances of his sarcasm are found in 1 Cor. 14.36; 2 Cor. 11.19, 5; 12.11 (in the latter two instances if the 'superlative apostles' were not genuine apostles the phrase is intended sarcastically). Teachers and parents are always told not to use sarcasm but Paul was a controversialist as well as a parent and his tongue may have run away with him; he had been severely provoked on all these occasions.

If Paul sometimes failed in respect of sarcasm he avoided another pitfall. He never talked down to his readers. He may say that they are not yet ready for a full spiritual diet (1 Cor. 3.1-3) but he does not use 'baby talk'. If they are his children they are grown children and not babies and he uses the arguments which are used with grown people.

Maturity and obedience

There are many ways in which parents and teachers seek to get their children to do what is right. We have explored some of them. One significant method remains, that of the direct order or command. Clearly there are occasions when there is no other possible way to act: 'Don't touch that pot or you will be burnt'. As we have seen the parental image in contemporary society was of a father[35] who gave orders to his household even when his children had grown into adults. We should not be surprised when Paul behaves similarly towards his converts. While he would certainly have viewed the ultimate obedience of his converts as offered to God he can view himself as the one through whom that obedience should be offered. Thus though he speaks in 2 Cor. 10.5 of taking 'every thought captive to obey Christ' he can go on in the next verse to speak of himself 'being ready to punish every disobedience'.

At another point in the same letter he says: 'this is why I wrote, that I might test you and know whether you are obedient in everything' (2 Cor. 2.9). Here the context indicates that Paul has in mind obedience to himself and not directly to God or Christ (cf. 2 Cor. 7.15; 1 Cor. 16.1, 'so you also are to do'). The Corinthians may have been difficult converts and have caused Paul special problems but the same cannot be said of the Philippians; to them Paul wrote 'Therefore, my beloved. as you have always obeyed, so now, not only as in my presence but much more in my absence ...' (Phil. 2.12). The obedience mentioned here is offered to Paul in respect of what he has said in 2.1-5 and picks up the obedience of Christ in 2.8. Writing in conciliatory fashion to Philemon as he sends back Onesimus he says: 'Confident of your obedience, I write to you, knowing that you will do even more than I say' (v. 21). Obviously he feels he can demand obedience but tactfully avoids it; in v.20 he puts the issue into the perspective of Christ. In relation to circumcision and slavery he says 'This is *my* (note not *the*) rule in all the churches' (1 Cor. 7.17). He tells the Corinthians that he will give *directions* about outstanding matters when he visits them (1 Cor. 11.34) and he reminds the Thessalonians of the

49

instructions he had given them while with them (1 Thess. 4.2; cf. 4.11; 2 Thess. 3.6, 14, 15).

In respect of 1 Thess. 4.1-12 C.H. Dodd comments

> There are several points here that should be observed ... First, there is the downright peremptory tone which Paul adopts. He neither argues nor offers tactful advice. He gives "orders"; the term which he employs is the term which is used for army orders... Thirdly, we can hardly be wrong in identifying these "orders" to which the apostle refers, as belonging to the regular course of ethical instruction for converts.[36]

Now while a good case can be made out that in 1 Thess. 4.1-12 Paul may be quoting the general catechetical teaching of the church this cannot be said of some of the other passages we have quoted for they are tied to Paul's judgement of particular situations.

Believers of course are not only Paul's children but children of God. In Gal. 4.1-7 he contrasts the position of his Galatian converts before and after they became Christians. As unbelievers they were no better than slaves from whom total obedience was to be expected. As Christians they are sons and daughters of the house, no longer in bondage but free. Their freedom is from the law and from the powers that previously ruled their lives. In the remainder of the letter Paul explains the nature of that freedom. It is one to be worked out in willing love. Does Paul offer the same freedom to his spiritual children? If he seeks obedience from them as their father is he demanding more than God demands from Paul himself and from all who have become Christians? Having set them free from the Jewish law does he impose a new law upon them. There is here both a wide problem and a restricted one. The wide problem, with which we shall not deal for it is essentially a problem in Pauline theology, asks whether Paul is imposing on his converts a new law when he seeks their obedience. Does this imply a conflict with his teaching on justification through grace alone? The narrow problem asks whether a father like Paul is really setting his children free and enabling them to mature when he prescribes their conduct.

The answer cannot be straightforward and simple. Young children need to be restrained from acting in particular ways for fear of harming themselves. Later as they grow up reasons can be given them for and against particular courses of action. The situation facing Paul is complex. His converts are adult in age and mental understanding but young in the faith. He himself comes from a faith, Judaism, which has had to face and solve many of the problems, e.g. in relation to idolatry, which they have to face. But Paul has also been a Christian for a considerable number of years and is mature in the faith. There may be times then when he will simply have to instruct his converts on the implications of their faith for the way they live. If he had always entered into a full discussion with them as to their conduct his letters would have become too lengthy; he needed to make his points as succinctly and sharply as possible; too much was at stake. So sometimes he simply has to ask for obedience to himself, though since he is God's representative the obedience is offered through him to God. But there will also be times, and the longer they are Christians the more increasingly this will be true, when he reasons with them. We have already seen how in many ways he treats them as mature, e.g. in presenting his views in the form of a reasoned argument.

More often than ordering his converts to do something he appeals to them. Philemon was Paul's son in the faith and he could have been 'bold enough in Christ to command' him 'to do what is required, yet for love's sake' he prefers 'to appeal to' him (vv. 8-9). He began by *directing* the Corinthians to take up a collection for the poor in Jerusalem. Later we find him reasoning with them, appealing to them and advising them to do the same thing (2 Cor. 8.8,10; 9.4). The tone of command has disappeared. Precisely why he changed that tone we do not know but we can presume he did so because he found an appeal more effective than a command. He prefaces many of his ethical instructions with words like 'entreat, urge, beseech, appeal'. While he was with the Thessalonians he had given them 'instructions' on sexual behaviour, an area on which as a Jew he would have had a very different outlook from that of their pagan upbringing; now writing to them he does not command them to keep his instructions but beseeches and exhorts them (1 Thess. 4.1-2; cf. 4.10; 5.12,14). In this he likens his own attitude to that of a father in exhorting and encouraging his children (1 Thess. 2.11-12; cf. 1 Cor. 4.14). When Euodia and Syntyche fell out with one another he did not *order* them to be reconciled to one another; that would have been impossible; instead he pleads with them (Phil. 4.2,3). There are even occasions when he confesses that he has no command to give his readers but only offers his opinion 'as one who by the Lord's mercy is trustworthy' (1 Cor. 7.25).

He regularly employs in this connection the word *parakalein*. This has a number of meanings, 'urge, entreat, console', etc. In the secular world it was also used at times as part of a formula.[37] When kings approach cities or communities which have some measure of independence but are not completely free they 'entreat' that city or community. It is thus a more tactful word than 'order'. Paul uses it in relation to the communities he has founded (1 Cor. 1.10; 4.16; 16.15-16; 2 Cor. 10.1-2; 1 Thess. 4.10-12; 5.14). He may not have been a king but he was Christ's ambassador (2 Cor. 5.20) and therefore possessed 'royal' rank. When he writes to the Roman church, a community he had not founded, this is his approach. He issues no commands to it.

Christ formed converts

We have drawn parallels between the way parents bring up their children and the way Paul brought up his converts. But there are significant points at which the parallel breaks down. In Gal. 4.19 Paul fears he may have to go into labour a second time over the same converts; no woman ever had labour pains twice over the same child. More importantly the life of an ordinary child is a continuation of the life of its parents; the life of Paul's converts was not a continuation of Paul's life. Paul's labour pains did not lead to the implanting of his life in his converts but the life of Christ, 'My little children, with whom I am again in travail until Christ be formed in you' (Gal. 4.19).

Paul knows that his converts have been born to a life other than his own. He did not choose to use the rebirth imagery as John does but in other ways he stresses that in the life of the convert there is something entirely new: 'if any man is in Christ, he is a new creation (creature)' (2 Cor. 5.17). We do not need to discuss the nature of that new life. A few passages will remind us of what is important. Christ is formed in the converts when they become Christians (Gal. 4.19). As they behold 'the glory of the Lord' they are 'being changed into his likeness from one degree of glory to another' (2 Cor. 3.18). They are baptised into the death of Christ 'so that as Christ was raised from the dead by the glory of the Father' they 'too might walk in newness of life' (Rom. 6.4). They learn to yield their members no longer to unrighteousness but themselves to God as those who have been brought from death to life (Rom. 6.13). At baptism they received the Spirit (1 Cor. 12.13) who does not kill but gives life (2 Cor. 3.6). They live no longer in the flesh but in the Spirit (Rom. 8.9); the Spirit helps them in their weakness (Rom. 8.26). Incidentally as those who posssess the Spirit they are able to recognise the truth of what Paul teaches (1 Thess. 4.8); they have themselves been taught of God (1 Thess. 4.9; cf 2 Thess. 3.4-5).

Paul may look on his converts as his children but he never expects them to invoke him as 'Abba, Father' (he thus fulfils Matt. 23.9 whether he knew it or not). God alone is to be

53

invoked in this way. Paul calls on God in precisely the same way as his converts. As children of God he and they are together fellow heirs with Christ (Rom. 8.15-17; Gal. 3.26-27; 4.6-7).

If Paul seeks maturity in his converts and if in a sense they are his children and if he regards himself as in some way mature he will look in them for a maturity like his own. So as we shall see in our next chapter he sets himself up as someone to be imitated. Paul owes his own maturity not to himself but to Christ. In him Christ is being formed. His maturity is not the gradual appearance of inborn capabilities which had long lain hidden but had been brought to light by good educational techiques. His maturity has its pattern outside himself in Christ and he receives from outside the grace and power that enable him to copy that pattern. In the same way the maturity that Paul as a good parent wishes to see in his children is not the drawing out of their innate abilities but the formation of Christ within them. He does not however believe that he himself has yet acheived full maturity.

> Not that I have already obtained this or am already perfect (mature); but I press on to make it my own, because Christ Jesus has made me his own. Brethren, I do not consider that I have made it my own; but one thing I do, forgetting what lies behind and straining forward to what lies ahead, I press on toward the goal for the prize of the upward call of God in Christ Jesus. Let those of us who are mature be thus minded.... Brethren, join in imitating me (Phil. 3.12- 17).

If Paul himself is not fully mature then neither will his converts be and he sets for them the same goal as he sets for himself.

Opening windows

Paul as the parent of his converts offered them much more than instruction in the Christian life and belief. He gave them a position before God. Each convert already had a position within a household as parent, child, slave, freedman (or woman). But this was not enough. It was a time of a changing and uncertain religious situation. The old traditional civic religions were losing their value and being replaced by new cults. People were not sure where certainty was to be found. Paul gave his converts a new and sure foundation. They were God's sons and daughters for whom Christ Jesus had died. The secret of existence had been imparted to them (1 Cor. 2.7-10). They were members of the holy people whose existence could be traced back in the purpose of God to Abraham, and in those days there was great respect for what was ancient. Unlike those around them they were 'sons of light and sons of the day' (1 Thess. 5.5). They formed a new community and each had a place within it as a member of the Body of Christ. In that way Paul provided them both with a base from which they could grow and a framework within which growth would take place.

But he did more. He opened to them new vistas of what life could be. He set before them new goals. He offered them a pattern far beyond what they had dreamed was possible:

> Whatever is true, whatever is honourable, whatever is just, whatever is pure, whatever is lovely, whatever is gracious, if there is anything worthy of praise, think about these things (Phil. 4.8).

And if that might seem touched and inspired by contemporary ethical ideals as well as Christian he held before their eyes the love of which he sang in 1 Corinthians chapter 13. He could open up windows in unexpected areas. Into a reasoned discussion of why the Corinthians should contribute more generously to the collection for the poor saints of Jerusalem he drops a kind of bombshell: 'For you know the grace of our Lord Jesus Christ, that though he was rich, yet for your sake he became poor, so that by his poverty you might become rich' (2 Cor. 8.9). Suddenly the whole way in which charity is to be conceived is transformed and given a wholly new perspective and Paul sets before his converts an inexhaustible model for action in many areas.

There are many other ways in which he inspires his readers. Though the final verses of Romans chapter 8 were not written to converts they might well have been. 1 Cor. 3.21-23 was and in it Paul opens the eyes of his converts to the true wealth of their new position as Christians:

> all things are yours, whether Paul or Apollos or Cephas or the world or life or death or the present or the future, all are yours; and you are Christ's and Christ is God's.

2 Cor. 4.16-18 was also written to converts:

> So we do not lose heart. Though our outer nature is wasting away, our inner nature is being renewed every day. For this light momentary affliction is preparing for us an eternal weight of glory beyond all comparison, because we look not to the things that are seen but to the things that are unseen; for the things that are seen are transient, but the things that are unseen are eternal.

There are times when we have to be critical of some of the methods Paul employs to assist his converts to mature, times when he even appears to forget temporarily that this is his main task. But when we look at the wider picture we can forgive the few blotches and wish that we ourselves had been his spiritual sons and daughters.

Notes

1. See especially P. Gutierrez, *La paternité spirituelle selon saint Paul*, J. Gabalda, Paris, 1968, pp. 199-232.
2. Cf. G. Schrenk, *T.D.N.T*, V, pp. 948-51.
3. W.K. Lacey, *The Family in Classical Greece*, Thames and Hudson, London, 1968, p.21.
4. J. Declareuil, *Rome the Law-Giver*, Greenwood, Westport, Conn., 1970, pp. 94-5.
5. Ibid. p. 95.
6. Lacey, op. cit., pp. 106-7.
7. Schrenk, op. cit., pp. 949-50.

8. *de Decal*, 120 (L.C.L. Translation).

9. S. Safrai in S. Safrai and M. Stern, *Compendia Rerum Iudaicarum ad Novum Testamentum: The Jewish People in the First Century*, vol. 2, Van Gorcum, Assen, 1976, pp. 771.

10. Cf. Sir. 30.1,2,13; Josephus, *c. Apionem* 2.206,217; *Ant.* 4.264; Philo, *de Spec. Leg.* 2.232.

11. Gutierrez, op. cit., pp. 173-5.

12. Cf. Safrai, op. cit., pp. 770, 947.

13. Translations as in G. Vermes, *The Dead Sea Scrolls in English*, Penguin, London, 1962.

14. Translation as in Soncino edition. Cf. Gutierrez, op. cit., pp. 44-9. See also H.L. Strack and P. Billerbeck, *Kommentar zum Neuen Testament aus Talmud und Midrasch*, München, 1922-8, Vol. 3. pp. 340-1.

15. Cf. J.H. Elliott, *A Home for the Homeless*, Fortress, Philadelphia, 1981, pp. 175-9.

16. A.J. Graham, *Colony and Mother City in Ancient Greece*, Manchester University Press, Manchester, 1964, pp. 40, 161-2.

17. iii.22,81 (L.C.L. Translation)

18. Cf. Gutierrez, op. cit., pp. 54-70; R. Reitzenstein, *Die hellenistischen Mysterienreligionen*. 3rd edn. Teubner, Leipzig, pp. 40-1.

19. Cf. Holmberg, op.cit., pp.79-80.

20. The reading *nēpioi* though it has good support involves a sharp change of metaphor within the verse. It would make Paul first describe himself and his associates as 'babes' and then as 'nurses' (mothers) taking care of babes. For a fuller discussion see Best, *A Commentary on the First and Second Epistles to the Thessalonians*, ad loc.

21. V.P. Furnish, *II Corinthians* (Anchor Bible), Doubleday, New York, 1984, p. 368 (italics his).

22. The use of male and female images together is also found elsewhere, e.g. 1QH 7.20-2; 9.34-6.

23. Cf. A.J. Malherbe, 'Gentle as a Nurse', *Novum Testamentum*, 12 (1970) 203-17.

24. There is some doubt as to the word used in Gal. 4.19 for 'children', either *teknia* or *tekna*. The latter is to be preferred. The former would indicate younger children and be more suitable to the 'mother' role and is therefore probably a correction. It is not otherwise used by Paul.

25. See n.20.

26. Allen, *Missionary Methods*, p.90.

27. On the wider use of the 'family' metaphor by Paul see D. von Allmen, *La famille de Dieu: La symbolique familiale dans le paulinisme*, Editions

Universitaires, Freiburg, Suisse and Vandenhoeck und Ruprecht, Göttingen, 1981.

28. See pp. 20, 73, 88-90, 148

29. When Luke depicts Paul as following Jewish tradition and appointing elders (Acts 14.23; cf.20.17) he is reflecting an 'office' which apparently existed from an early period in the church in Jerusalem and was probably more widespread in his own time. There is no trace of 'elders' in any of the genuine Pauline letters.

30. Cf. Allen, op.cit., pp. 174-6, 131.

31. Cf. N.R. Petersen, *Rediscovering Paul: Philemon and the Sociology of Paul's Narrative World*, Fortress, Philadelphia, 1985, pp. 65-78, 291-4.

32. Cf. W.G. Doty, *Letters in Primitive Christianity*, Fortress, Philadelphia, 1973. See the letters in 1 Macc. 10.18-19,25-26; 14.21; 2 Macc. 9.19.

33. Cf. Petersen, op. cit., p.72.

34. G. Shaw, *The Cost of Authority*, Fortress, Philadelphia, 1983, pp. 30,67, suggests such terms are used to flatter but he does not apparently accept them as true statements.

35. See above pp. 31-4

36. C.H. Dodd, *Gospel and Law*, Columbia University Press, New York, 1951, pp. 13-14.

37. Cf. C.J. Bjerkelund, *PARAKALŌ*, Universitetsforlaget, Oslo, 1967.

III

PAUL AS MODEL

Whether wholly true or not there is some truth in the old adage 'Like father, like son'. There may then be some appropriateness in moving from considering Paul as father of his converts to looking at the way he makes himself their model.[1]

Imitation of Christ

Paul says to the Corinthians 'Be imitators of me, as I am of Christ' (1 Cor. 11.1; cf 1 Thess. 1.6). This provides a control over what it means to imitate Paul: in the final issue it is imitation of Christ. The origin of Paul's idea of the imitation of Christ has been variously traced to Judaism, gnosticism, the mystery religions and Greek philosophy. We do not need to discuss this since we are concerned solely with the way in which Paul uses the idea.

It has also been hotly debated when Paul thinks of the imitation of Christ whether he has in mind imitation of the earthly Jesus or imitation of the incarnate and crucified Christ. Certain passages, e.g. the Philippian hymn (2.6-11,[2] 2 Cor. 8.9; Rom. 15.3,7) suggest the latter. Paul it is said tells us so little about the life of the earthly Jesus that it is difficult to see how he could have set him before his converts as a model. Yet there are other considerations. Paul does not leave his converts in entire ignorance of Jesus; he quotes sayings which he attributes to him (1 Cor. 7.10; 9.14); he recalls to them Jesus' last supper. Many allusions to, if not direct quotations of, Jesus' teaching have been found in his letters. In the Philippian hymn Paul says that Jesus was obedient not just to death but to 'death on a cross', a phrase which it is widely believed he himself added to the hymn. The cross was not then simply a mythical or

59

supernatural event for Paul but a real happening. If it has become symbolic for us it was too actual and horrible a method of execution in the ancient world for Paul's converts to think of it in any other way than as something which required love on the part of Jesus. When Jesus is described as 'servant' or 'slave' in the hymn this would also awaken overtones in converts many of whom were slaves.

When we look more closely into what Paul wrote we can see at various points how he depends in his argument for an understanding of the dying love of Jesus. After detailing some of what he himself suffered he speaks of 'always carrying in the body the death (lit. 'dying') of Jesus ... so that the life of Jesus (note the double use of the personal name) may be manifested in our mortal flesh' (2 Cor. 4.10-11). When he writes of a daily dying (1 Cor. 15.31) he has in mind something like the dying of Jesus on the cross. Some narration of how Jesus actually died must have been included in what Paul told his converts. When then he spoke of imitating Jesus he could draw on this.

This is not to say that the 'mythical' element in which the Son of God becomes man should be eliminated from the picture nor that imitation is the only way in which Paul expresses the relation of himself and other believers to Christ. They have been buried with Christ into his death (Rom. 6.4,5). Christ is in them (Gal. 2.20) and they are in Christ (2 Cor. 12.2). They are members of Christ's Body, the church, are being transformed by the Spirit into the image of Christ (2 Cor. 3.18), and are new creations (creatures) in Christ (2 Cor. 5.17). We should also note from this that there are areas in which Paul cannot imitate Christ. He was never crucified for the sins of humanity, nor were his converts ever baptised into him (1 Cor. 1.13).

Origin of the idea of the imitation of Paul
Paul did not think up this idea for himself. Imitation of others was a widespread theme in the contemporary world.

1. It is regularly used in relation to sons and fathers. Isocrates exhorts Demonicus to follow the example of his father Hipponicus saying

> I have produced a sample of the nature of Hipponicus, after whom you should pattern your life as after an ensample, regarding his conduct as your law, and striving to imitate and emulate your father's virtue.[3]

Imitation of the father extended to imitation of the 'fathers', i.e. the fathers of the people or nation. This is found in Judaism: 'Remember the deeds of the fathers, which they did in their generations' (1 Macc. 2.51).

2. It is used of the relation of subjects and rulers, good subjects imitate their rulers. According to Xenophon, Cyrus the Persian ruler

> believed that he could in no way more effectivley inspire a desire for the beautiful and the good than by endeavouring, as their sovereign, to set before his subjects a perfect model of virtue in his own person.

Xenophon goes on to say that

> the rest of the Persians also imitated him [Cyrus] from the first; for they believed that they would be more sure of good fortune if they revered the gods just as he did who was their sovereign and the most fortunate of all.[4]

3. Pupils were expected to imitate their teachers.[5] Dio Chrysostom in writing of the relation of Socrates to Homer says

> Then if a follower he would also be a pupil. For whoever really follows anyone surely knows what that person was like, and by imitating his acts and words he tries as best he can to make himself like him. But that is precisely, it seems, what the pupil does-by imitating his teacher and paying heed to him he tries to acquire his art.[6]

Seneca says the same and draws out some of the reasons why disciples should imitate their teacher

> Of course, however, the living voice and the intimacy of a common life will help you more than the written word...

Cleanthes could not have been the express image of Zeno, if he had merely heard his lectures; he shared in his life, saw into his hidden purposes, and watched him to see whether he lived according to his own rules. Plato, Aristotle, and the whole throng of sages who were destined to go each his different way, derived more benefit from the character than from the words of Socrates.[7]

Quintillian brings out the same point of the need to associate with the teacher if there is to be effective imitation

For however many models for imitation he may give them from the author they are reading, it will still be found that fuller nourishment is provided by the living voice, as we call it, more especially when it proceeds from the teacher himself, who, if his pupils are rightly instructed, should be the object of their affection and respect.[8]

Quintillian also argues that the character of the teacher is critically important.[9]

Damis, the disciple of Apollonius of Tyana, joined him saying, 'Let us depart, Apollonius, you following God and I you.'[10] Here we have the twofold imitation that we find in Paul (1 Cor. 11.1; 1 Thess. 1.6).

4. The good are to be imitated. 'If there are men whose reputations you envy, imitate their deeds.' 'Be not satisfied with praising good men, but imitate them as well.'[11] This idea appears in Jewish as well as in Greek literature: 'pattern your life after the good and pious man Joseph... See then, my children, what is the goal of the good man. Be imitators of him in his goodness because of his compassion, in order that you may wear the crown of glory.'[12] Martyrs are of course included in the category of good men and so the first of the seven martyred brothers says to the others 'Imitate me.' (4 Macc. 9.23;[13] cf. 2 Macc. 6.27-8).

In this kind of cultural environment it is not surprising that Paul's converts should find it natural to imitate him. They would look on him as their father and teacher, and model for Christian conduct. They were accustomed to the distinction between precept and example and there is no need to see in Paul's call to imitate him merely a veiled call to obedience to his instructions.[14] We move on then to examine the passages in which Paul uses the idea (we cannot restrict our discussion to the appearance of the word alone) of imitation of himself.

1 and 2 Thessalonians

In his earliest letter, 1 Thessalonians, Paul does not call on his readers to imitate him but points out that they have already been doing so.[15] In 1.5b he says that they know the kind of people he, Silvanus and Timothy were when they brought the gospel to Thessalonica and lived among them. The three had suffered persecution both when they became Christians and afterwards in their evangelism. His readers would have learned this not only from the three themselves but also from their fellow Christians in Philippi and Beroea (Acts 16.11-40; 17.13-15). The Thessalonians in their turn had suffered when they became Christians and as they lived as Christians. Christ had fulfilled his destiny in suffering; Paul, Silvanus and Timothy had suffered and so had the Thessalonians. The latter in turn had become an example to other Christians:

> You know what kind of men we proved to be among you for your sake. Amd you became imitators of us and of the Lord, for you received the word in much affliction, with joy inspired by the Holy Spirit; so that you became an example to all the believers in Macedonia and Achaia (1 Thess. 1.5-7).

Paul saw himself and his companions as an example to the Thessalonians not in suffering alone but also in loving. In the prayer which ends the first part of the letter he writes 'may the

Lord make you increase and abound in love to one another and to all men, as we do to you' (3.12).

Paul and his companions had also provided another and quite different example of true behaviour, which was especially relevant to those needing to be steadied in time of apocalyptic expectation. Some had given up their daily work to prepare for the return of the Lord. Paul reminds them: 'you yourselves know how you ought to imitate us; we were not idle when we were with you.' As an apostle he had the right to maintenance from them but he had forgone this 'to give you in our conduct an example to imitate' (2 Thess. 3.7,9). If Paul worked so should they.

1 and 2 Corinthians

Paul sets himself out as model several times in this correspondence. The principal passage is 1 Cor. 4.6-21 where as we already indicated[16] he presented himself as the father of his converts. As we have also seen imitation and sonship were closely connected in the ancient world. Paul first touches on the idea of imitation in v.6 (this is a notoriously difficult verse but the difficulty lies outside our area of interest). He is drawing to an end his discussion of the parts played by the various leaders in the church and writes 'I have applied all this to myself and Apollos for your benefit, brethren, that you may learn by us...' In vv. 12-13a he then contrasts his own behaviour, and probably also that of Apollos, with that of at least some of the Corinthians: 'When reviled, we bless; when persecuted, we endure; when slandered, we try to conciliate'. When he behaved in this way Christ was his model (cf 11.1). He goes on to remind them that he is their father and continues: 'I urge you, then, be imitators of me' (v. 16). This is followed up by saying that he had earlier sent Timothy to them 'to remind' them 'of my ways in Christ' (v. 17). In biblical speech the ways of a man are more than his ethical instructions; they are the ways in which he lives. Timothy is to recall Paul's life to the Corinthians. He can do this because he is Paul's 'beloved and faithful child in the Lord' (v. 17) and sons reproduce the conduct of their fathers. Within the immediate context Paul's ways would be the manner in which he accepted injury in Corinth not merely without protest but conciliating and blessing in return (vv. 12,13). In the wider context of the discussion of wisdom and group rivalries in chapters 1-4 Paul's ways correspond in weakness to the weakness of the cross. Imitation of Paul should then be imitation in suffering. This was also the area of imitation we discerned in 1 Thess. 1.6. We shall find it recurring in Phil. 1.30.

Paul of course does not require imitation of every detail of his life. He desires others to resemble him in celibacy but he does not demand that everyone should practice celibacy: 'I *wish* that all were as I myself am ... To the unmarried and the widows I say that it is well for them to remain single as I do' (1 Cor. 7.7-8). Paul recognizes that there are limits to imitation, limits created by the kind of people we are ('if they cannot exercise self-control', v. 9) and the situation in which we are already involved (celibacy is impossible for those who are married!).

At 11.1 Paul parallels imitation of himself and of Christ, 'Be imitators of me, as I am of Christ.' The preceding chapters have prepared the way for this for in them he has regularly referred to his own conduct in respect to financial independence (9.1-23) and to eating or abstaining from food which had been sacrificed to idols (8.13). He brings everything to a head in the three verses leading to 11.1 where he says

> So, whether you eat or drink, or whatever you do, do all to the glory of God. Give no offence to Jews or to Greeks or to the church of God, just as I try to please all men in everything I do, not seeking my own advantage, but that of many, that they may be saved. Be imitators of me, as I am of Christ (10.31 - 11.1).

65

In relation to food Paul is willing to adapt himself to the company he is with. In particular though he believes there is nothing sinful in eating food which had been sacrificed to idols he will forgo this if it offends others or causes them doubts over the faith. Christ did not please himself (cf. Rom. 15.2,3); Paul does not please himself; his converts ought to follow him in this. 'Be imitators of me, as I am of Christ' (1 Cor. 11.1). There is just one other point in the letter where Paul points to his own behaviour as a guide to the Corinthians-in respect of speaking in tongues (14.6,19). He desires the Corinthians rather to seek spiritual gifts which like his would edify the church more deeply.

Paul makes no explicit reference to imitation of himself in 2 Corinthians though there are constant allusions to his behaviour when he was in Corinth (1.12,17; 2.17; 4.2; 7.2; 10.2,10; 11.5-7; 12.11-13,17). After he wrote 1 Corinthians and prior to his writing of any part of 2 Corinthians, Paul's conduct had been vigorously attacked in Corinth. It would therefore have been pointless for him to present himself to the Corinthians at this stage as an example. If they regard him as a rogue he would not wish them to copy him in his alleged roguery. He himself has of course no doubts about the correctness of his conduct (2.14-17; 3.2; 6.3-10; etc.).

Galatians

This letter may be as polemical as parts of 2 Corinthians but in it Paul is refuting attacks not so much on his character as on his gospel and apostolic position. He can therefore set out his own conduct as an example to others. He writes: 'Brethren, I beseech you, become as I am, for I also became as you are' (4.12).[17] How has Paul become like the Galatian Gentile Christians? By rejecting all dependence on the Law for his claim to salvation. He has surrendered all those advantages to which as a Jew he had laid claim before his conversion. His converts however are in danger of falling back into the clutches of legal requirements. They 'observe days, and months, and seasons, and years'; Paul is afraid he has 'laboured over' them 'in vain' (4.10,11). They must imitate him in depending on Christ alone (4.12). From another angle he has provided them with an example of true Christian freedom.[18]

Philippians

Here Paul again uses the theme of imitation, and at one point in a way not unlike that in which he had used it in Galatians. In 3.17, 'join in imitating me, and mark those who so live as you have an example in us', the sphere of imitation must lie in the immediate context. There Paul has been speaking of his readiness to lose everything in which he had once had confidence, of his desire to know Christ in the power of his resurrection and of straining forward to obtain the prize of the upward call of God in Christ Jesus (3.3-16). Interestingly within this he speaks of himself 'becoming like him [Christ] in his death' (v. 10); the element of Paul's own imitation of Christ is then also present.

Imitation is also the theme of 4.9, 'What you have learned and received and heard and seen in me, do.' This follows directly on a picture of ideal Christian behaviour, 'whatever is true, whatever is honourable, whatever is just, whatever is pure, whatever is lovely, whatever is gracious, if there is any excellence, if there is anything worthy of praise, think about these things' (4.8). It is in this the Philippians are to follow him. Finally the idea of imitation lies in the background of 1.29,30, 'it has been granted to you that ... you should ... [be] engaged in the same conflict which you saw and now hear to be mine'. If the Christian life is to be depicted as a struggle then Paul has himself provided the pattern of the way to wage and win it.[19]

Conclusions

From this brief survey of passages where Paul introduces the theme of imitation we see that the call to copy him is never set in completely wide and unfettered terms; it is always linked to the context of his argument at the point where he issues the call and is restricted to named areas of conduct. Though there are many areas in which he would like others to take him as their example there are limits to what he asks. He never summons his converts to leave all and go with him in full-time missonary work as Jesus did (Mark 1.16-20). Indeed while he summons them to imitate him he never summons them to follow him (again contrast Jesus in Mark 2.14; 10.21). He does not expect his converts to have similar visionary experiences to his (2 Cor. 12.1-10). If married he does not call on them to break up their marriages and live in celibacy. There are however aspects of his character and work which they can and should follow. Most importantly there is the acceptance of salvation through Christ and the continued dedication of life to Christ.

He only calls churches which he had founded to imitate him. Their members have been able to observe him. So the Roman Christians are not summoned to copy him, though they are to imitate Christ (Rom. 15.2,3). Even if the Romans know little of Paul they can be expected to know something of Christ.

Is Paul arrogant in summoning his converts to imitate him? As we have seen the call to imitate parent, teacher, ruler, good man was a regular theme in the ancient world. In the literary evidence which has come down to us the call is mostly made in the third person, i.e. it is good to take your teacher, parent or ruler as example. 4 Macc. 9.23 and 2 Macc. 6.27-8 are clear exceptions in that the speakers seek imitation of themselves. But mostly it is not the parent, teacher or ruler who says it directly to those in his or her charge. Yet people then were much like what they are today and it is hard to believe that parents and teachers would not from time to time have said to their children and pupils 'Imitate me'. When also teachers say that teachers should be imitated it is difficult to believe that they excluded themselves as examples. To say this however does not completely remove the charge of arrogance. That many people perform an action does not make it right nor is the ethos of contemporary society necessarily correct.

As we approach the question of Paul's arrogance we do well to note that the first reference to imitation in his writing is not an exhortation to imitate him but a statement that the Thessalonians have already done so. It cannot be proved but it is not inconceivable that it was the Thessalonians who first raised the matter of imitation by telling Paul that they had been using his life as an example. He may then have taken up the theme and suggested to others that they should imitate him. Whether this is so or not there are two ways in which the charge that Paul was arrogant may be softened.

(1) Paul believed that he himself imitated Christ. He says this explicitly in 1 Cor. 11.1 and 1 Thess. 1.6 and it is implicit in other passages, e.g. 1 Cor. 4.17, 'my ways in Christ'. He stresses the need to imitate Christ at other points without any reference to himself (Phil. 2.5-11; 2 Cor. 8.9; Rom. 15.2-3). Thus the imitation of Christ is primary. Moreover where Paul does speak exclusively of imitation of himself this relates as much to 'salvation' (Phil. 3.17; Gal. 4.12) as to moral conduct.

(2) Paul regularly refers to the imitation of others and not only of himself. In the Thessalonian passages he writes in the plural including Silvanus and Timothy with himself as patterns to copy (1 Thess. 1.6; 2 Thess. 3.7-9; so also he includes Apollos with himself in 1 Cor. 4.6). At Phil. 3.17 after calling for imitation of himself he continues, 'mark those who so live as you have an example in us', probably referring to prominent Christians in the church at Philippi. More strikingly in 1 Thess. 2.14, where in the context of suffering he might have referred to his own suffering, he refers instead to that of the churches in Judea. He holds up before both the Corinthians and the Macedonians the conduct of the other (2 Cor. 8.1-5; 9.2) in

69

relation to their contributions to the collection for the poor saints in Jerusalem. The apostles and the brothers of the Lord are examples in respect to maintenance by the churches (1 Cor. 9.5) though Paul does not follow their example. Israel can function negatively as an example (1 Cor. 10.1-12). Paul therefore sees imitation as more than imitation of himself alone.

We should also recall the unique place Paul believed he occupied in the plans of God.[20] He was the last to have seen the risen Lord; he had received his gospel in a distinctive way; he was the apostle to the Gentiles. If there is any truth in this, more importantly, if Paul believed there was truth in it, then it is not unnatural that he should set himself out as example before others.

It is important to remember the positive value of example. Many of Paul's contemporaries stressed this.[21] When Paul went to a fresh city and proclaimed the gospel of the Saviour's loving descent from heaven and his redeeming death on the cross this was so far outside the normal experience of love that if that love was to be understood it required not only to be spoken of but also to be exemplified in a life lived out before the new converts. The distance between Paul's story of the love of God in Christ and normal experience could be bridged only by an actual example of a loving life. A recital of incidents in the life of the historical Jesus could not convey the meaning of his behaviour with the same force as someone living at least partially like him.[22] In our own day in many mission fields it has been the way the pioneers have displayed the love of Christ in their lives that has been the most powerful agent in showing converts how they themselves should live.

In addition to the question of Paul's possible arrogance we must inquire whether he was worth taking as an example. Our answer is bound to be linked to our estimate of his arrogance. If this was a major factor in his character we shall necessarily regard him as less worthy of imitation. If it was not then we shall more readily view him as someone to copy. Lacking independent evidence other than what Acts provides his character is difficult to assess. Yet no matter what our conclusion in respect to it there was no one else apart from his associates whom his converts could imitate. Certainly in so far as we consider he exercised a reasonable measure of true fatherly care over his converts we will regard him as worthy of imitation. That is not to say Paul was perfect; we have seen deficiencies in the way he has treated his converts and we shall see more, though not major deficiencies. However Paul's character is not our direct concern.

Notes

1. While much has been written on the imitation of Christ there has been less study of the imitation of Paul. The principal examination is that of W. P. De Boer, *The Imitation of Paul*, J.H. Kok, Kampen, 1962. See also Gutierrez, op. cit., pp. 175-188; J.H. Schütz, *Paul and the Anatomy of Apostolic Authority*, Cambridge University Press, Cambridge, 1975, pp. 226-232; D.M. Stanley, ' "Become imitators of Me" ', Apostolic Tradition in Paul', *Biblica* 40 (1958), pp. 859-77; idem, 'Imitation in Paul's Letters. Its Significance for His Relationship to Jesus and to His Own Christian Foundations' in *From Jesus to Paul: Studies in Honour of Francis Wright Beare* (ed. Peter Richardson and John C. Hurd), Wilfred Laurier University Press, Waterloo, Ontario, 1984, pp. 113-26.
2. We are not concerned about the origin or original meaning of this hymn.
3. *To Demonicus* 4.11 (L.C.L. translation).
4. *Cyropadeia* VIII 1. 21,24 (L.C.L.translation).
5. Cf. B. Fiore, *The Function of Personal Example in the Socratic and Pastoral Epistles* (Analecta Biblica), Rome 1986, pp.33-5
6. *Discourse* 55.4,5 (L.C.L.translation).
7. *Epistulae Morales* VI 5-6 (L.C.L. translation).
8. Quintillian, *Inst.'* 2.28 (L.C.L. translation).
9. Quintillian, *Inst.*, 2.1-8.
10. Philostratus, *Life of Apollonius*, I. 19 (L.C.L. translation).
11. Isocrates, *To Nicocles* 22.38 and 38.61 (L.C.L. translation).

12. *Testament of Benjamin* 3.1; 4.1 (translation as in J.H. Charlesworth, *The Old Testament Pseudepigrapha*, Doubleday, New York, 1983-5, vol. I, pp. 825-6).

13. See Charlesworth, op. cit., vol. II (1985), p. 555.

14. So Michaelis, *T.D.N.T.*, IV, pp. 663-73; his views have been widely rejected.

15. Patte, op.cit., p. 133, plays with words when he says that the Thessalonians are imitators, not because they follow Paul's example, but because the same things happened to them as to him. Presumably they happened to them as consequences of behaving in the same way as Paul (Patte finds it difficult to be consistent in this matter, cf. pp. 142, 152). Generally speaking Patte sees the type/imitator pattern as basic in Paul's relations with his converts. We see this pattern as part of the wider parent/child pattern. The type/imitator pattern excludes the reciprocal and is therefore incomplete as a model for Paul's relation to his converts. Paul is much more than a type to his converts (the leader of a group of free mountain climbers, as Patte puts it, p. 235); he is a father and a source of authority.

16. Above, pp. 35-7

17. While the precise translation of this verse is uncertain its main meaning is not in doubt.

18. Cf. G. Lyons, *Pauline Autobiography: Towards a New Understanding* (SBL Dissertation Series 73), Scholars Press, Atlanta, Georgia, 1985, pp. 171-2.

19. For the sake of completeness we mention Acts 20.33-5 where in his speech (see above pp. for discussion of the speech) to the Ephesian elders Paul may be regarded as setting himself out as a model. The area of imitation is restricted to that of leaders not accepting maintenance from the church. This is an area in which we do not find Paul seeking imitation in his letters. Indeed he elsewhere recognizes the right of leaders to maintenance (1 Cor. 9.3- 18).

20. See above pp. 8-11

21. See the quotations from Dio Chrysostom and Seneca on pp. 61f

22. See Fiore, op. cit., pp.89-97 for self-description as example.

IV

EXERCISING AUTHORITY[1]

That Paul exercised some kind of authority over the churches he founded is shown in that he wrote letters to them and sent his assistants to instruct and advise them. The nature of that authority and how he exercised it is another matter. In the models of relationship under which Paul dealt with his converts it is difficult to introduce the idea of authority into those of a reciprocal nature for Paul does not allot himself a special position in the Body of Christ. The father however was, as we saw in chapter II, a figure of authority in the ancient world. In one of the principal passages where Paul uses this model he ends by speaking of coming to the Corinthians with a rod (1 Cor. 4.15,21). The master builder for his part controls the whole structure. This model, unlike that of the parent, allows for the exercise of subordinate authority under the master builder. When Paul employs it (1 Cor. 3.10) he extends it to work done by others and in the context specifically mentions Apollos. He does not however mention local indigeneous leaders.

Every organisation possesses some authority structure. Even in the simplest of groups leaders rapidly emerge. Decisions have to be made and a forceful figure is soon found to be making most of them. During his initial mission in each church Paul would have occupied a special position in relation to decision making. Even after he left he appears to have still wished to continue his leadership. Day to day decisions must also have been made in his absence. We do not know a great deal about these and who as leaders made them. We have no need to explore this since we are only concerned with Paul's exercise of authority. But we should note that when Paul asks the local community to decide about something he addresses it as a whole and does not operate through leaders within it (1 Cor. 5.3-5).

People come to positions of authority in differnt ways and exercise their authority differently. We are accustomed to a democratic model in which leaders are elected for a period and then changed through due procedure. Paul certainly never regarded himself as the elected leader of his churches. He viewed his leadership from one point of view as their founder, from another as the one whom God had chosen to minister to them. Thus his belief that he can speak with authority comes out even when he is not specifically referring to his call by God (cf. 1 Thess. 2.4,13).[2] His position in relation to his churches was then very different from that of pastors who are chosen by their congregations and who at least theoretically can be dismissed by them or a superior ecclesiastical body. Paul also was never in the position of needing to bestow favours to woo a sensitive electorate.[3]

Some authoritarian structures like those of the armed services or large corporations operate through chains of command. Those below are expected to execute without deviation the orders of those above. Those who rise to higher rank are normally groomed for this and appointed to it by those above them. This did not happen in Paul's case; indeed probably those like James who already held authority initially opposed Paul. The hereditary model in which authority passes from one generation to the next by lineal descent is also very different from Paul's position. But other factors in his upbringing may have prepared him in part for the exercise of authority. If, as is probable, he came from a wealthy family, from an early age he would have been in a position to order others about. His training as a rabbi may have contributed. In some societies where 'holy men' are reverenced they train younger people to succeed them and instil in them the idea that they are in some

74

way different from their fellows. If this happened during Paul's training in the interpretation of the Law then once he became a Christian he lost all the eminence he had gained from that training and in particular from being a pupil of Gamaliel. The controlling group of apostles and elders in Jerusalem did not say to themselves after his conversion: 'Saul is a good man; he has been both trained in the Law and understands the Greek world; he would get on well with people: we need to extend our area of operations; let's appoint him as our representative in the Hellenistic world.' In Galatians Paul hotly rejects any idea that he is the representative or appointee of any human group.

Some come to positions of eminence and authority through their own personal qualities. A Socrates attains his ascendancy over his disciples through the power of his mind. A Henry Ford heads his business and makes it succeed through his inventive ability and enterprise. Everything we know about Paul before and after his conversion suggests he did not lack the elements of drive and intellect that would have led him to rise in any society. He was no colourless personality elevated by chance into a position he could not maintain on his own.

Leaders of large organisations and governments choose their subordinates in at least two ways: fearing a palace revolution and their own overthrow they may surround themselves with those who will work submissively exercising little personal initiative or they may choose those whom they see to have genuine ability to carry on after their (the leaders) own death or retirement. If we regard God as Paul's leader he did not pick a nonentity but a man of vigour whose vigour, suitably guided, could be used.

In any individual case it is difficult to disentangle the actual factors which lead to a particular person coming to power. Training, education, being born with a silver spoon in the mouth, initiative, vigour all have their part to play and are

75

combined in varying proportions in different leaders. Paul had many of the advantages which would have brought him into a position of responsibility wherever he was. Added to his natural advantages was his vehement belief that God had called him to a special position in the church. But when as a leader in it he began to exercise authority how much of that authority in practice derived from God and how much from his upbringing and the force of his own character? No simple answer can be given. We can say neither that Paul was merely God's rubber-stamp nor that he was just a human being of very strong and insistent character.

The basis of Paul's authority

A possible approach would be to outline the teaching of Jesus on authority ('I am among you as one who serves'; Luke 22.27) and see if Paul exercised his authority in that way. Instead we begin by seeking the bases on which Paul rested his authority.

If authority is not to be exercised in a purely arbitrary manner then those who exercise it and those over whom it is exercised must have some common ground. There needs to be a certain reasonableness on both sides. In a democracy this requires that rulers and ruled have an equal respect for the rule of law and that the ruled recognize the right of rulers to rule. In a college it requires that teachers and students have an equal respect for truth, that students recognize the superior prior training and knowledge of their teachers and that teachers recognise the desire for truth on the part of their students. When Paul preached in a city those who became Christians left one authority structure and joined another. The common bond which made possible the new authority lay in both his and their recognition that they had the same Saviour and accepted the same faith. At the same time Paul as the initial proclaimer of that faith and Saviour could expect what he said to be accepted and his instructions and advice to be heeded.

Paul regularly stresses the common bonds linking him with his converts through his use of the first person plural in important statements. This appears when he expresses the faith: 'We shall not sleep, but we shall all be changed ...'(1 Cor. 15.51); when he reminds them of their joint need to avoid sin: 'We must not indulge in immorality ...' (1 Cor. 10.8; cf. 10.9); when he pleads with them to act in the same way: 'Let us, therefore, celebrate the festival...' (1 Cor. 5.8). Both he and they are subject to the same judgement: 'We must all appear before the judgement seat of Christ' (2 Cor. 5.10).

When we turn to inquire more precisely into the bases Paul chose on which to rest his authority we can immediately eliminate one possibility, letters of recommendation. When people travel they often take such letters with them from friends at home to the friends of their friends overseas. Paul was at one time troubled by those who came to Corinth bringing such letters (2 Cor. 3.1). When he himself went to Corinth, or any city for the first time, he had no letters of introduction. (He could write them; Philemon is one.) There would have been no one to whom he could have presented them. From where then did he derive his authority?

1. There are preachers who preface all their assertions with 'The Bible says'. How often and in what ways did Paul use his Bible, the Old Testament? It was certainly a bond linking him with his converts. Does he then assert his authority on the basis of what can be read in that book? Sometimes, but not often. (Note that in asking this we are not asking how much of the content of what he said was derived from the Old Testament.[4]) Occasionally when setting out the 'rules' to which Christian behaviour should conform he quotes:

> Beloved, never avenge yourselves, but leave it to the wrath of God; for it is written, 'Vengeance is mine, I will repay, says the Lord'. No, 'if your enemy is hungry, feed him; if he is thirsty, give him drink; for by so doing you will heap burning coals upon his head' (Rom. 12.19f).

The 'rules' however commence at v.9 and the vast majority of them are unsupported by any reference to the Old Testament. In the instructions about the mingling of believers and unbelievers in 2 Cor. 6.18-20 we have a catena of sayings drawn from the Old Testament but this is unusual.[5] Sometimes we have only brief references to that book in the middle of longer and other arguments (1 Cor. 6.16; 9.9; 14.21; 2 Cor. 8.15; 10.17; 13.1). Very often Old Testament quotations are used to verify conclusions reached on other grounds. It is only in Galatians and Romans that Paul uses the Old Testament in a sustained way. He probably does so because in both letters the argument is about an Old Testament concept, the law, and he is refuting opponents who have based their arguments on it.

2. Paul also appealed to what was generally accepted as good in contemporary society; here he shared common ground with his readers. This appeal is part of his argument about the 'dress' of men and women at worship (1 Cor. 11.13-15; cf. Rom. 1.26-7) and of his judgement on incest (1 Cor.5.1). The behaviour of Christians should at all times be such that anyone will recognise it as good (1 Thess. 4.12). The works of the flesh are obvious to anyone (Gal. 5.19-21). In 1 Cor. 15.33 he quotes a common proverb. He can also simply set the record straight in respect of the facts when he details why he changed his plans to visit Corinth (2 Cor. 1.23 - 2.4). In every case here he is arguing as would anyone, Christian or unbeliever.

3. We might expect Paul to share with his readers a common respect for the teaching of Jesus and to sustain his advice to them on its basis. Twice (Rom. 13.9; Gal. 5.14) he uses the levitical command (19.18) about loving one's neighbour. On neither occasion does he appeal to the Old Testament; more surprisingly he does not appeal to Jesus' use and extension of it to all men. Perhaps he assumes his converts know all this. But if so he certainly does not put the authority of Jesus explicitly behind what he says. In fact there are very few occasions when

he does this. He refers explicitly to Jesus in relation to divorce (1 Cor. 7.10), to the financial maintenance of apostles (1 Cor. 9.14) and to the final consummation (1 Thess. 4.15-16; this last may be a saying of the exalted Lord delivered through a prophet but it is still treated as coming from Jesus). Paul also uses the words of Jesus when instructing the Corinthians on the celebration of the Eucharist, though he introduces the material as tradition he has received rather than as part of the teaching of Jesus. Other passages suggest Paul knew more of the teaching of Jesus than these few instances reveal.[6] However he makes no explicit reference in them to Jesus and so does not consciously put Jesus' authority behind his use of them. There is no reason to suppose his readers would necessarily have seen in them an appeal to that authority. It is important to remember in this connection that much of the moral teaching of Jesus was good Jewish teaching. Paul would first have heard the Golden Rule (Matt. 7.12) in its negative form as part of the teaching of Rabbi Hillel. It and other teaching would not then be fixed in his mind as the teaching of Jesus and he may have felt no need to pass it on as such.

In addition to this many of the situations for which Paul's advice was needed were different from those that faced Jesus. There would be no sayings of Jesus which he could use to lend weight to his counsel. Paul can quote Jesus about divorce in general but he cannot quote him in respect of a marriage between a believer and a pagan; so when he comes to this section of his discussion of divorce he begins 'I say, not the Lord'(1 Cor. 7.12). He could not draw on the teaching of Jesus about food sacrificed to idols because Jesus as a Jew living among Jews had no need to comment on that subject. Jesus had never collected money for others and so there was no saying of Jesus which Paul could use to give authority to what he said about the collection for Jerusalem. There were then many situations for which neither the teaching of Jesus nor that of the

Old Testament could provide the necessary basis for Paul's authority.

Though Paul quotes a saying of Jesus in 1 Cor. 9.14 he does not apply this saying to himself; he refuses the financial assistance it commends.[7] If he is not himself bound by the teaching of Jesus can he expect others to be bound? It might be logical to answer 'No!' but people are not always logical. Paul must have seen special circumstances which led him to modify or disregard this particular saying. Does he allow sufficently for his converts in their special circumstances to modify or disregard his own instructions? When parents are criticised by their children they often reply: 'What you say is all right, but you are to do as I say for I know better than you'. Paul knows better than his children. He was more certain that he possessed the mind of Christ than that they did (see 6 below).

4. Paul and his converts shared the common tradition of the church. He appeals to it when instructing the Corinthians about the Eucharist (1 Cor. 11.23-6) and when using confessional material (1 Cor. 15.3, 'I delivered to you as of first importance what I also received ...'). In relation to the dress of women praying and prophesying in church he says 'If any one is disposed to be contentious, we recognise no other practice, nor do the churches of God' (1 Cor. 11.16; cf. v.2 and 14.33-4). He also employed common catechetical material in ethical instruction; this can be detected in Rom. 12.9-21 and 1 Thess. 5.1-11. His readers would recognise it as such and would not regard it as based on his personal authority. In a similar way he also uses common theological material (e.g. Phil. 2.6-11) which he does not need to refer to as such because his converts already know it.

It is generally accepted that he modifies this latter christological hymn by the insertion of 'even death on a cross' (v. 8). He may also be responsible for the addition to the account of the Eucharist of 'as often as you eat this bread and drink the cup, you proclaim the Lord's death until he comes' (1 Cor. 11.26). Various suggestions have been made as to the way in which he modified the little creed that underlies Rom. 1.3-4.[8] In his training as a rabbi he had studied some of the ways in which the Torah was extended and modified to meet new problems. Now that he was a Christian the tradition of the church would have occupied in his mind the same place as the Torah and equally require updating and modification.[9]

5. It may be said that Paul derived his authority from his position as an apostle, a position recognised by his converts. But his apostleship was not without its critics even among his converts and could not be easily taken as common ground. We have also seen that Paul did not stress his apostolic position when he came to counsel and instruct his converts.[10] If he proceeds from any position in his advice and instruction it is from that of 'founder of the church', the spiritual father of his converts. Since the father in the ancient world was an 'authority figure' it was natural that Paul should exercise authority. We have already seen how he looked for the obedience of his converts who were his children.[11]

6. If however the exercise of authority is appropriate to parents, they normally act within an accepted range of what may or may not be demanded of children. The limits are set by society. For Paul's converts the new 'rules' of the church were very different from those to which they had been accustomed. They were that even to Paul. He could not simply bring along the rules of Jesus, of the Old Testament, of existing church tradition and apply them. Some could be applied but Paul and his converts were continually facing new situations which required new 'rules'. Paul and his converts were into a new game that had not been previously played and Paul had to write new rules for it. He had of course been playing the game much longer than any of his converts and could move from a developed theological position into new situations.

But what right has Paul to create new rules? On what basis can he do so? From where does he get his understanding of what is really going on in the new game? His developed theological position can be detected by studying his letters. His approach to his converts is however more immediate. He is the spiritual man who 'judges all things ...', who has 'the mind of Christ' (1 Cor. 2.15-16). He is not one who teaches what people like to hear (1 Thess. 2.3-4) but teaches as a man 'of sincerity, as commissioned by God', as one who 'in the sight of God' speaks 'in Christ' (2 Cor. 2.17; cf 12.19). His words are the word of God (1 Thess. 2.13; cf. 4.8). He instructs, as he says, 'through the Lord Jesus'(1 Thess. 4.2; cf. 5.27), though in the verses that follow he does not quote Jesus nor seem to depend directly on his teaching. When he rebukes the Cor-inthians he refers to Christ as speaking in him (2 Cor. 13.3). The Corinthians for their part should acknowledge that what he writes to them about glossolalia, prophecy and the conduct of worship is 'a command of the Lord' (1 Cor. 14.37). Paul's claim of course relates to a much wider area than that of ethical instruction alone. From the beginning of his work in a city God spoke through him (1 Thess. 2.13). His gospel is not man's gospel; no human had taught him it; it had come to him through a revelation of Jesus Christ (Gal. 1.11-12). He is an ambassador of Christ (2 Cor. 5.18-20).

It is this belief that Christ speaks through him that above all else enables Paul to meet the new situations which face his converts. Where there is no word of the Lord about mixed marriages he supplies rules (1 Cor. 7.12-16) thus modifying Jesus' teaching on divorce. Jewish teaching on the importance of marriage had also become inadequate for Paul because of the nearness of the return of Christ; so he says in relation to celibacy 'I have no command of the Lord, but I give my opinion as one who by the Lord's mercy is trustworthy' (1

Cor. 7.25). He has then continually to devise ways to deal with new problems.

The passages at which we have been looking usually contain some reference to Christ or the Spirit, as if Paul claimed their authority and backing for what he said. There are however times when this reference disappears. Writing about the collection he says 'as I directed the churches of Galatia, so you also are to do' (1 Cor. 16.1). There are other passages where he seems 'to lay down the law'.

> Whoever, therefore, eats the bread and drinks the cup of the Lord in an unworthy manner will be guilty of profaning the body and blood of the Lord (1 Cor. 11.27). If any one has no love for the Lord, let him be accursed (1 Cor. 16.22; cf Gal. 1.9).
> If any one destroys God's temple, God will destroy him (1 Cor. 3.17).

The same tone of voice appears in the rules he gives for the conduct of worship (1 Cor. 14.13,28,30). The origin of these statements has been examined closely; they have been regarded as the product of apocalyptic Christianity [12] or as deriving from Jewish Wisdom literature.[13] It is not necessary for us to determine what influenced Paul in writing them. We are concerned rather with their peremptory nature and the absence of any reference to Christ or the Spirit. Ignatius of Antioch at the beginning of the second century noted this characteristic when he wrote 'I do not order you as did Peter and Paul'.[14] We still hear today the same peremptory tone of voice in some preaching, especially in that of a denunciatory nature. There we can observe the certainty with which preachers will declare certain human activities (e.g. dancing, alcohol, a marxist analysis of society) as incompatible with being a Christian.

In relation to passages like those we have just quoted Ladd says 'Paul lays claim to an understanding of the mind and will of God that on the purely human level is close to arrogance'. [15] He goes on to point out that Paul speaks like this because he is conscious of being called by God to a position of apostolic authority.[16] It is true as we have noted that Paul on most occasions refers to Christ or the Spirit as the source of his authoritative statements. Is this reference to be extended to all of them? A doubt will always linger because in the course of the history of the church there have been many who spoke with the same vehement authority as Paul but later turned out to have been self-deceived. When Paul answered the criticism that he was not a true apostle he described his opponents as false apostles and went on to say 'for even Satan disguises himself as an angel of light' (2 Cor. 11.14). His opponents had a false confidence. May what he sees as a danger for them not have been a danger for himself? It must have been. Was he aware of it? He was, for there are passages in which he says he has no certain 'word of the Lord' and offers instead an opinion, 'I give my opinion as one who by the Lord's mercy is trustworthy' (1 Cor. 7.25; cf v.40 and 2 Cor. 8.8). He also recognises that he is as subject to God's final judgement as any of his converts or opponents (2 Cor. 5.10; 1 Cor. 4.6) and will therefore have to account for his over confident statements if Christ was not behind him in making them.

There is one other aspect to which attention should be drawn. Those who give pastoral advice are regularly faced with situations for they which they can find no direct help in Scripture or in the tradition of the church. If they are to give effective help they may often find it necessary as they counsel to speak with a greater assurance than they actually feel. Luther once said of Paul when Paul was being advanced as a model to follow: 'I don't think (Paul) believed as firmly as he talks. I cannot believe as firmly, either, as I can talk and write about it'.[17]

What happens when two people each of whom claims to speak in the name of Christ clash in respect of what they say? Generally Paul's authority as father of his converts meant that he did not run into this kind of difficulty from them. But he did have opponents. In Chapter VI we shall see how he dealt with them and learn that he did not simply assert his own point of view.

To sum up: Paul saw his authority as deriving from the Old Testament, from what was accepted in society, from the teaching of Jesus, from the tradition of the church; all of which had to be adapted to new situations. His ability to adapt came from his relationship to Christ and the guidance he received from the Spirit. His confidence in giving new instructions came also from Christ and the Spirit and from his special relationship to his converts as their 'father'. There is an immediacy about his authority that resembles that of the prophets of the Old Testament and which must have been present in the words of the New Testament prophets. Of course he does not always speak with this 'immediate' confidence. As we saw in Chapter II he often argues, putting forward a reasoned case.[18]

The limits of authority

Authority is seen not only in determining the truth and in telling people how they ought to behave but also in the way people are controlled. Here it clearly works within limits. Paul recognised this when he divided responsibility for evangelisation with the Jerusalem leaders. His sphere was that of the Gentiles, theirs that of the Jews.[19] It may be that he recognised further limitations within the Gentile sphere. He does not build on the foundations of other missionaries (Rom. 15.20). When he and Barnabas split up (Acts 15.39) Barnabas must have had his own area. Paul never evangelised N. Africa but flourishing churches quickly appeared there, probably within his lifetime. We do not know who were their missionaries.

There are however limits on authority other than those of race or geographical area. In the judicial systems of many countries lower courts can only impose fines up to a certain sum or imprisonment up to a limited period. Crimes meriting more severe punishment go to higher courts. Paul does not appear to have regarded his authority as restricted in any way as to penalty. However we understand the trial of the incestuous man and Paul's part in it (1 Cor. 5.3-5) the sentence is not less than excommunication. While Paul sees himself here as acting in some way together with the church and the Holy Spirit, in 2 Cor. 13.2 ('if I come I will not spare them') he threatens to act on his own.

In Acts 5.1-11 Peter pronounced the death sentence on Ananias and Sapphira because they had cheated the church over their contribution to it when they sold their property. There is no reason to suppose Paul would have acted differently. He shows no signs of agitation when some who treated the Eucharist without due respect fell ill or died. He excommunicates those who in Galatia preached a gospel different from his own (Gal. 1.8-9). In the ancient world the father had great power over his family and Paul was the spiritual father of his converts. [20] There is no reason suppose he envisaged any limit to the extent of his authority.

Paul sometimes acted alone in exercising authority; at other times he sent one of his associates, Timothy or Titus to sort out a difficult situation. On occasions he summoned the local church to work with him. At no time though he recognises the existence and authority of local leaders (1 Cor. 16.16; 1 Thess. 5.12) does he call on them to take action. It may be that although there were a number of people in the community who possessed some authority there was not suffcient local acceptance of their position for Paul to use them. His own authority ought to be acceptable to everyone. Paul did not then see any limit placed on his own authority by the existence of a local leadership. He might perhaps have been glad to see its emergence for when some members of the Corinthian church had a disagreement and went outside the church to have it settled he laments that 'there is no man among' them 'wise enough to decide between' them (1 Cor. 6.5). There are wider questions relating to the nature of Paul's leadership and we shall return to them in Chapter VIII.

The purpose of authority

Authority can be exercised with various ends in view. Some exercise it for self-aggrandisement and enjoy its exercise, and few who have authority would deny that there are not moments when they enjoy their position. That Paul does not reveal any such moments does not mean that he did not have them; they are not the kind of thing one writes about to those regarded as immature. Paul however argues his sincerity (e.g. 1 Thess. 2.1-12); those who are sincere are not normally in the business of self-aggrandisement.

There are two main puposes for which authority is used: to maintain the status quo (its sole purpose according to the 'law and order' school of thought) and to initiate change and development. The same person can pursue both these ends, though at different times. When people came to the Galatian churches seeking to overturn Paul's teaching on the Law he used his authority to maintain the status quo of his own teaching. But when he first went to the Galatians he had used his authority to initiate them into ways that had never before been theirs. His whole gospel was new to his converts and in continuing to draw out its implication for them his authority was used to change their lives.

Another aspect of the purpose of authority comes out in a phrase Paul himself uses. It can be used both to build up and to destroy (2 Cor. 10.8; 13.10; the phrase comes from Jer. 12.16-17). Paul tells the Corinthians that God has given him the power to do either but that he would rather build up than destroy. Though he does not there use these terms the same preference is evident in the context of 1 Cor. 4.21, 'Shall I come to you with a rod, or with love in a spirit of gentleness'. One of the reasons he writes to the Corinthians is to avoid the need to come and discipline them. The subsequent course of his dealing with them shows that he did not need to use the rod at that moment.

The two references to building up or destroying fall in the final section of our second letter to the Corinthians. This is probably the last surviving portion of his correspondence with them and so we do not learn from Paul himself the outcome of his discipline. Since his letter still exists we can assume the Corinthians did not tear it up (Paul did not keep a carbon or photo-copy!) and reject his authority. That the church continued to exist and that when Clement of Rome [21] wrote to it towards the end of the first century he could quote Paul to it leads to the same conclusion: the church had been built up rather than destroyed. If as some scholars hold these chapters (10-13) belong to an earlier, now lost, letter to the Corinthians then clearly the conclusion is the same for chapters 1-9 would then be Paul's final letter to them and in it he is on reasonably good terms with them.

When Paul speaks of building up he has in mind the community as much as particular individuals within it. The purpose of his discipline is both to restore errant individuals and to heal the entire fellowship.[22] When someone falls into sin it is not only that individual who suffers but the whole community, the Body of Christ. When a member has to be excluded it is not only the member who suffers but the whole Body. To cut off one member of one's body is to harm one's whole self.

We may be disquietened because Paul envisages part of his activity as destructive rather than as therapeutive. If he had found it necessary to carry out his threat of destruction what would this have entailed? In 2 Cor. 10.4-5 he writes of the destruction of the arguments of his opponents and this is perfectly natural; 10.8 and 13.10 however refer to the destruction of people. The contexts of these passages throw little light on what that destruction would involve. The opposite term is 'build up' and Paul uses this more frequently; from it we may learn something of what 'to destroy' may have meant. Paul employs the metaphor of building up in relation to charismatic gifts which should be used to benefit the church as a whole and not for the self-glorification of the user (1 Cor. 14.4,5,17; the R.S.V. reads 'edify' here but the Greek word is the same). Love builds up (1 Cor. 8.1). Those who are weak in the faith are built up when those who are strong do not please themselves in relation to what to eat and to holy days (Rom. 15.1-2). To build up then is to assist the church to mature in its faith and practice so that it will grow closer to its Lord. To destroy must be the opposite: to remove from the church and the hope of salvation those who have erred from their faith and closeness to Christ.

Yet when Paul counselled the exclusion of the incestuous man from the Corinthian church he did not go as far as to deny the possibility of his salvation (1 Cor. 5.5). He is disciplined but not destroyed. There is no actual case of discipline where we can be sure Paul gave up someone to destruction. Yet when he lays a curse on those who preach a gospel other than his own (Gal. 1.8-9) he comes near to seeking their destruction. Those who have been cursed can hardly hope to remain close to Christ or to reach a happy end to their faith! When then Paul spoke of coming to Corinth with the possible intention of destroying those who had withstood him and his gospel (2 Cor. 13.1-10) he may have had in mind the laying of a curse on them. If this seems to belong to a world other than that in which we live so also are the statements that his opponents will strike on the face those who do not accept their ways (2 Cor. 11.20) and that some have fallen ill and some died because they participated irreverently in the Eucharist (1 Cor. 11.30). The attitude of mind which accepts these as normal would not stumble at a curse working eternal consequences.

What we have in 2 Cor. 10.8; 13.10 is only a threat. We cannot assume that Paul would actually have put a destructive curse on the Corinthians. They themselves accused him of being humble (i.e. obsequious) when with them but full of courage (bravado?) when far away and writing letters (2 Cor. 10.1). It is hard to believe that Paul was two different people in that kind of way. It is more likely that threats he might make when absent he found it much more difficult to execute when faced with those who had erred. Present with them he would then become more aware of the consequences of what he had threatened and in sympathy draw back from extreme action. It is true that he threatens future punishment from God (Rom. 2.5,8,16; 5.9; 12.19; 1 Cor. 3.13-15; 2 Cor. 5.9-10; 1 Thess. 5.9) but that is not the same as threatening to make his own judgement about who should be punished and deciding the nature of the punishment.

If in his attempt to sustain his authority Paul's ultimate threat was excommunication did he also make promises of blessing? His letters do not contain promises of the joys of heaven to those who accept his decisions, but then he may not have needed to make such promises since all his readers believed that faithful Christian service resulted in such joys. Certainly Paul did not go around saying, 'If you obey me and are good Christians God will prosper you now on earth and you will be rich and successful'(2 Cor. 9.6-11 appears to be the only exception). His own life, as that of his Master, was too much of a contradiction of any such view.

We may be taking here too narrow a view of blessing. In biblical terms it is the opposite of cursing. Yet just as cursing may seem a little strange to us so may blessing. To bless in the ancient world was not merely to utter a pious wish for another's well-being; it was to pass on some positive good.

While Paul refers several times to the need to bless there is only one type of occasion where he says he does so himself: 'when reviled, we bless' (1 Cor. 4.17). He might however also be said to bring a blessing to his converts when he healed them and this could be viewed as an exercise of authority especially in the case of exorcism. (We have to go to Acts for actual accounts of his healings but passages like 2 Cor. 12.12; 1 Thess. 1.4-5 confirm what we read in Acts.) Paul of course does not claim the power to heal as his own; it came to him from God.

Authority through knowledge
People exercise power and authority through the knowledge they possess. Teachers exercise it over students by imparting or withholding from them the information needed to pass examinations. The expert lays claim to authority through his knowledge: it is not for the layman to make judgements on the safety of nuclear generation of electricity! When Paul first arrived in any of his churches he had a knowledge that none of his hearers possessed: he knew the gospel and he had a grounding in the Jewish faith; on the basis of both he was equipped to make judgements in theology and ethics. Despite this advantage there is no sign that he surrounded his knowledge with a mystical aura in order to keep others from understanding it. In his letters he is always attempting to explain what he knows and relate it to his converts' situation. Nowhere does he say 'here is something too deep for you to understand'. He only once withholds information; this related to what he saw and heard in his rapture to the third heaven. Here (2 Cor. 12.4) it was neither unwillingness on his part nor incapability of understanding on the part of his readers that kept him silent but a divine command not to speak.

As time went by others (e.g. the Fourth Evangelist) might appear with as profound, even a more profound, understanding of the gospel than Paul but his letters do not suggest he

91

believed there were any who had done so while he was alive. He was however vulnerable at one point: he had never been a disciple of the earthly Jesus. This inadequacy seems to have been exploited by some of his critics. (In Chapter VI we shall see how he fought off these and other critics.) In response he could at least make the claim to have met the risen Jesus.

In Corinth there was a group which believed its members had a superior knowledge not open to all Christians. The existence of this group led Paul to expound his understanding of wisdom and therefore of knowledge (see 1 Corinthians chapters 1-4). In his discussion he relates knowledge to power and both to the cross. The wisdom of the cross and the power of the cross are not the wisdom of this world and its power. This being so, the knowledge of the cross can never confer upon its possessors a superior form of knowledge only to be shared grudgingly, if at all, with others. The wisdom of the cross is not a secret doctrine into which some believers are initiated at a time later than conversion. There is no aspect of knowledge of the cross which is withheld from some Christians so that those who possess it may feel superior to those who do not.

Knowledge may give its holder power over others; so also can the manner in which it is presented. People can be talked into a course of action or thought through specious arguments dressed up in fine words. The power of knowledge can also be exercised through demagoguery. Paul's rejection of a special knowledge is accompanied by a rejection of the skills and tricks that speakers normally use to persuade others (2 Cor. 10.10; 11.6). This does not mean that he could not write and speak with both passion and eloquence. I Corinthians 13 and Rom. 8.31-9 show he could do both. It does not mean that Paul rejected all the methods of rhetoric taught in the ancient world for he uses many of them from time to time. He can use syllogistic argument (2 Cor. 3.17; Gal. 3.20; 1 Thess. 4.14), metaphor and analogy (Gal. 3.15; 4.1; 1 Cor. 15.35-41), allegory (1 Cor. 9.9-10; 10.3-4; Gal. 4.21-31) and typology (1 Cor. 15.21- 22). He argues *a fortiori* (1 Cor. 6.2-3; 9.11-12), that one thing is true in order that another may be so (1 Cor. 11.19; Gal. 3.19; Phil. 1.25-6) or that something is done, or happens, to produce a particular effect (1 Cor. 7.2; 8.13; 2 Cor. 7.8; 12.7-10). He uses the style of the diatribe (Rom. 3.1-8; 9.14- 33).[23]

Paul employs all these traditional methods of argument and yet at the same time belittles his own intellectual approach (1 Cor. 1.17,20; 2.4-5,13; 2 Cor. 1.12; 2.17; 11.6). It is in fact impossible to present an argument without the use of some rhetorical tools even if the user is is unaware of their use. Paul however did not set out to use them for their own sake, to appear learned or skilled in speaking, nor through their use to manipulate his readers and flatter their intellects. Only at a few points does he even appear to play on their emotions (1 Cor. 6.1-11).

Paul never leaves the impression that he is merely an advocate presenting a case or using words because they sound well or have an emotive effect. He passionately believes what he writes. Often his grammar breaks down to the despair of those who have to expound him. The verdict of his contemporaries was that 'his speech' was 'of no account' (2 Cor. 10.10); they regarded him as 'unskilled in speaking' (2 Cor. 11.6). Paul then can be acquitted of the charge that he used his knowledge in such a way as to lure his readers into making false decisions or true decisions made from the wrong motives.

As we leave the theme of Paul's exercise of authority it is perhaps wise to note that he lived in a more authoritarian age than ours. We who are accustomed to democratic ways have often difficulty in understanding those who are not. Had Paul not exercised his authority his churches would have fallen apart. They did not, but that does not mean that authoritarian ways are the ways for the church today.

Notes

1. On Paul's authority in general see Holmberg, op.cit.
2. See Helen Doohan, *Leadership in Paul*, Michael Glazier, Wilmington, 1984, p.43.
3. For other features in Paul's leadership see below pp. 140-5
4. For the aspect of content see V.P.Furnish, *Theology and Ethics in Paul*, Abingdon, Nashville, 1968, pp.42-4.
5. Some scholars believe Paul did not write 2 Cor. 6.14 - 7.1.
6. There is a reference also to the teaching of Jesus in the address to the Ephesian elders (Acts 20.35). Leaving aside doubts about both the genuinenss of the logion and the speech as Pauline we note that the saying is not used so much in the course of an argument as are the sayings in 1 Cor. 7.l0; 9.14; 1 Thess. 4.15-16 but as the climax of the speech. Paul's final words stress not his own example but the teaching of Jesus.
7. See below p. 99-104
8. See the commentaries.
9. See P. Richardson, ' "I say, not the Lord": Personal Opinion, Apostolic Authority and the Development of Early Christian Halakah', *Tyndale Bulletin* 31 (1980) 65-86.
10. See above pp. 18-20
11. See above pp. 48-52
12. So E. Käsemann 'Sentences of Holy Law in the New Testament' in his *New Testament Questions of Today*, S.C.M., London, 1969, pp.66-81.
13. So K. Berger, 'Zu den sogenannten Sätzen Heiligen Rechts', *N.T.S.*, 17 (1970/1) 10-40.
14. *Romans* 4.3 (L.C.L. translation).
15. G. Ladd, *A Theology of the New Testament*, Eerdmans, Grand Rapids, 1974, p.379
16. Ibid. p. 380.
17. *Tischreden*, II. 222, 19-23. Translation as in H.G. Haile, *Luther: A Biography*. Doubleday, Garden City, N.Y., 1980, p.305.
18. Above pp. 41, 48 and below pp. 92-4
19. It makes no difference if the division was made on geographical grounds rather than racial; in either case Paul recognises limits to his authority.
20. See above pp. 31-4 for the power of the father.
21. 47.1; cf. 5.5-7.

22. Cf Dean S. Gilliland, *Pauline Theology and Practice*, Baker, Grand Rapids, 1983, p.244.

23. For the ways in which Paul conducts his arguments see F. Siegert, *Argumentation bei Paulus*, J.C.B.Mohr (Paul Siebeck), Tübingen, 1985, pp.181-247.

V

PAUL AND MONEY

When money enters into the relationship between people it can exercise a disturbing if not disruptive effect. There were two major areas in which Paul became involved with his converts over money. The first was relatively straightforward in that he was seeking money for others; the second was much more difficult because it related to what he should be paid by his churches in respect of his own work in them. We commence with the former.

The collection

When Paul made his agreement with the leaders of the church in Jerusalem about his missionary work and the offering of the gospel to the Gentiles on the condition of faith alone they asked that the churches which he founded should remember the poor saints in Jerusalem[1]. He therefore organised a collection for these saints among those churches. The importance with which he viewed this collection can be seen both in the large place it occupies in his letters (two whole chapters of 2 Corinthians as well as briefer references in others) and in the way in which he was prepared to put his life in peril by himself bringing what had been gathered to Jerusalem (Rom. 15.31).

The two chapters (8 and 9) of 2 Corinthians are largely taken up with his appeal to the Corinthians to increase their contributions. Paul does not remind them of the agreement; he had no need to do so since he would have explained everything when he first introduced the subject; 1 Cor. 16.1ff implies that this was probably during his initial mission in the city. It is only in his letter to the Roman Christians that he offers an explanation; it was necessary in this case because he had not visited their church . He tells the Romans that the churches of Macedonia and Achaia had made their contributions because they believed they were in debt to the Christians of Jerusalem with whom the gospel began. Because Gentiles share in its spiritual blessings they should render a return. This they could do best by giving from their own material blessings (Rom. 15.26f). To us, accustomed to television pictures of famine from various parts of the world, it is curious that Paul presents no tear-jerking sketch of conditions in Jerusalem. Lacking any evidence to the contrary we must assume that what he said to the Romans represented his practice also when introducing the subject to the churches he founded. Such an approach is not out of keeping with the initial reference to the collection in Gal. 2.10 where it is seen as part of an arrangement or bargain between himself and Peter, John and James.[2]

When he had first been in Corinth he had instructed his converts to make regular weekly contributions (1 Cor. 16.2); this had apparently not worked as successfully as he had hoped and so when he wrote again (2 Corinthians chapters 8 and 9[3]) he reverts to the subject. In an attempt to set up a healthy rivalry he reminds the Corinthians how well the churches in Macedonia have contributed (8.1-7). He says that he is asking no more than that they should give in proportion to the wealth they have (8.11f). He tells them he fears that when the time comes to gather the various church contributions together the Macedonian believers may find that the Corinthians have not given very generously, and he, Paul, will be put to shame in their eyes (9.4). The Corinthians themselves will be blessed if they give generously (9.6-12). Their gifts are their opportunity to glorify God (9.13). Above all he reminds them how Jesus who was rich in heaven became poor on earth for their sakes; therefore they should be ready to become poor for the sake of others (8.9).

In all this we can sense some tension. It surfaces when Paul feels he may be put to shame by the failure of his own converts in a church where he had laboured so long (at least eighteen months according to Acts 18.11) in comparison with his much shorter periods in the churches of Macedonia. It surfaces at another point. There were many travelling teachers, philosophers and magicians who went from city to city, accepted fees for what they did and lined their pockets with no consideration for the truth of what they taught. The criticism that Paul preached only to improve his own financial position had probably appeared much earlier for we find Paul refuting it in his first extant letter (1 Thess. 2.5). In Corinth Paul may have been accused that he was only enthusiastic about the collection because a large proportion of it would never reach Jerusalem but go to his own support. Doubts about his honesty were probably increased because he accepted no money for his own maintenance from the Corinthians (2 Cor. 12.16). From where then did he get enough to live on? The auditing of accounts was unknown in those days so to clear himself of suspicion Paul says that independent observers will be appointed to receive the collection and transmit it to Jerusalem (8.16-24). He does not then either ride rough-shed over the criticisms that have blown up or ignore them but seeks in so far as it is possible to meet them and clear himself.

Paul's own maintenance

The second financial matter in which Paul became involved, support for his work of evangelism and its consolidation, proved to be much more damaging to his relations with his converts.

One of an apostle's acknowledged priviliges, if we may so term it, was the right to support when engaged in apostolic work (1 Cor. 9.3-18). Peter and others had exercised this right and Paul in discussing it not merely does not reject this right but even supports it with various arguments. The shepherd has the right to milk from the herd. The ox, according to the Old Testament, when treading out the corn should not be muzzled. The priests in the temple are entitled to some of the sacrifices. As a final justification Paul quotes Jesus to the effect that those who proclaim the gospel should get their living from it (1 Cor. 9.7-14). It was then perfectly legitimate for apostles to be supported financially by the churches to which they ministered. Yet Paul refused such support in Corinth and seemingly also in other areas (1 Thess. 2.9).

The arguments Paul uses clearly cannot be confined to the case of apostles. They imply that all who have full-time pastoral responsibility are entitled to financial help.[4] Paul does not argue the general case for he is only interested in the position of apostles but he appears to accept the wider implications in Gal. 6.6 where he argues that those who are taught should share 'all good things' with their teachers. 'All good things' is a very wide term and while it would include a sharing of whatever spiritual gifts those who were taught had received it would also include money and maintenance. We may suppose that Paul himself would have been ready to benefit in this way from his converts.

Yet Paul rejected maintenance and when he did so it was not simply from unselfishness. As we have just seen he impressed on the Roman Christians their need to contribute to the collection because they owed a debt to the Jewish Christians of Jerusalem. His converts owed him a like debt for without him none of them would ever have been Christians. Yet he never makes this point. When he preached the Gospel he did so not to put his converts in his debt but because compulsion was laid on him by God (1 Cor. 9.16-18).

Paul's behaviour in respect of support has always been a puzzle for it appears he accepted gifts of money from the Philippians when he had gone on to Thessalonica (Phil. 4.15,16). The Philippians, and probably also the Thessalonians, sent him money again when he was in Corinth (2 Cor. 11.9). It may be that he only accepted such gifts after he had left a community but took nothing from it while he was in it, for 1 Cor. 4.12, where he lists his labouring with his hands in parallel with various afflictions which continually affected him and were not restricted to a few communities, indicates a general practice. The practice may have varied in relation to some communities after he had been with them long enought for mutual trust to build up.[5] He could then allow them to support him.

In the ancient world when a teacher arrived in a new city there were four ways open to him to maintain himself: to charge fees, to beg, to work, to seek a wealthy patron.[6] Since Paul, coming to a new area, would not have been preceded by reports of his success as a teacher he would have been unable to charge fees. There is no indication that he ever begged though it would not have been out of accord with the instructions the Gospels report Jesus as giving to his original disciples (Mark 6.7-13 and parallels; Luke 10.1ff). While such a practice was possible in the restricted area of Palestine where the distances between villages were small this was no longer possible for someone who moved only from one large city to another and who had no time to preach and beg in every village on the way. We must assume that when Paul left one city he had enough in hand to support himself until he reached the next and could obtain work. It may well be that after preaching in a city some wealthy person would take him home and provide for his needs. Though there were wealthy people in his congregations Paul never refers to hospitality received from them apart from the mention of Gaius (Rom. 16.23). Since Romans was probably written from Corinth but not during Paul's initial mission we can assume that during one of his later visits he accepted part of his keep from one of the members. He had not however accepted support from the congregation as such. (The

101

visit during which Gaius was his host probably took place after the final four chapters of 2 Corinthians had been written.) Moreover it is not clear to what extent or in what ways Gaius was his host since he is also said to be that to all the church. If then Paul did not beg, charge fees or have a wealthy patron the only course open to him was to work.

As a young man he had learnt a trade connected with leather.[7] Opportunities for employment would exist in most cities. The tools required for leather work would be easy to carry around with him.[8] Working with others itself provided evangelical opportunities. Even more the open shops in which trade was carried on could easily lead to discussion with people passing by who might wish to question further the strange teacher they had heard in the market place.[9]

This brings us back to Corinth where Paul worked to support himself and where after he had left he was criticised for doing so. Peter, the brothers of the Lord, other apostles, or to be more exact, their supporters had claimed that apostles had the right to maintenance (1 Cor. 9.5). If then Paul did not exercise that right did this mean he was not an apostle?

Before we examine Paul's defence of his conduct we should recognise that he began his mission activity and decided on the way it should be carried out long before he came to think of himself as an apostle equal to Peter and others of the Twelve. [10] There was much in the ancient world to encourage him in a policy of self-support. From the time of Socrates it had been held that the truly wise man did not sell his wisdom for money.[11] It was also not unusual for Jewish learned men to be financially independent of those they taught. Though the Jewish rules for Rabbis in this respect were formulated at a slightly later period the idea may already have been 'in the air'.[12] Jesus again had never accepted maintenance.

While Paul might have been influenced by contemporary practice we should probably look for deeper reasons governing his conduct. It is noticeable that he introduces the question of support into his discussion of the 'strong' and the 'weak' in respect of food sacrificed to idols (1 Corinthians chaps 8-10).[13] The 'strong' may need to give up some of what they claim to be their right in order to show their love for their 'weaker' brethren. So Paul gives up the right to maintenance. This however sounds more like an argument devised to meet a particular situation than Paul's basic position.

As we have seen Paul regarded his place in God's plan of mission as unique. Should he therefore be beholden to any man for his mission activity? If he was maintained by his churches did he not nullify the grace of God through which all evangelisation took place? Here again his thinking ran along lines not unfamiliar to the ancient world. The Cynics taught self-sufficency and by earning his own living Paul was being self-sufficent (cf. Phil. 4.11, 'I have learned, in whatever state I am, to be content', *autarkēs*;[14] see also 1 Thess. 4.12). To receive money could also put one under an obligation to the giver.[15] Yet Paul was not motivated simply by the desire for self-sufficiency. If he was free he was also a slave-a slave to God and therefore also a slave to men (1 Cor. 9.19). A slave is not paid. When Paul preaches he is under the compulsion of God (1 Cor. 9.17). How then can he claim support for doing what he has no choice but to do? The Gospel must be free of charge (1 Cor. 9.18). His attitude to his converts is relevant here also. When he reminds the Thessalonians of the way he had laboured night and day among them he does so in the context that he is their father (1 Thess. 2.7-12). Fathers do not expect their children to work to support them (2 Cor. 12.14). Even more importantly his determination to work to support himself fitted into his life-style, a style which corresponded to that of Jesus in being one displaying weakness and foolishness (1 Cor. 1.18ff).[16] Only the important are supported by others.

If when Paul had originally worked out in his mind how a missionary like himself should behave in respect of payment he had taken such matters into consideration we can see how loath he would have been to surrender this position even if it led to doubts being cast on his apostleship. He would rather die than go back on his principles (1 Cor. 9.15). His offence was doubtless compounded in Corinthian eyes because while he took no money from them he had accepted gifts from the churches of Macedonia (2 Cor. 11.8-9). Yet whatever the objections Paul was not prepared to surrender his settled policy and if his main defence is offered in 1 Corinthians we see him returning to the subject in his later writing to the same church (2 Cor. 11.7-11; 12.13). The problem would not go away.

Paul does not accept money because he has no wish to put any obstacle in the way of the gospel (1 Cor. 9.12; cf. 2 Cor. 6.3). But has he not put a great obstacle in the way of its success in Corinth by his stubborn refusal to accept financial support? In the next chapter we shall look at how Paul dealt with the opposition he encountered there. For the moment we need only observe how settled principles, and apparently good principles, can lead to dissension. One wonders if Paul had forseen what was going to happen might he not have exercised a little more flexibility. And yet had he done so because of what happened in respect of the collection it is probable that he would have been at once accused of preaching and teaching for the money he could make out of it. There was no way in which he could win. To change his principles might indeed have been the worst thing he could have done.

There is one other and much smaller area where Paul became involved in financial matters. When he sent back the slave Onesimus to Philemon he promised to repay any loss Philemon may have suffered-if Philemon pushes him to it. He clearly does not expect to be pushed for he reminds Philemon how much the latter already owed him as his spiritual father (vv.18-20). Paul tells us neither the amount which might be owing to Philemon nor its cause. Perhaps when Onesimus ran away he had stolen from Philemon or by being away had deprived Philemon of the services to which as owner he was entitled (Onesimus had either purchased him or paid for his upbringing including his education). If Philemon had insisted on payment how could Paul have paid him? Paul as he wrote was in prison (v.1). He expects however to be released and he could then have worked and earned money. Perhaps instead he intended to pay for Onesimus out of the money sent to him by churches like those in Macedonia? We can only hope that Philemon did not demand cash down.

Notes

1. Whether the collection was intended for the poor among the saints in the Jerusalem or for all the saints (the poor) has been much debated but is not relevant to our discussion.

2. J. Paul Sampley, *Pauline Partnership in Christ* (Fortress Press, Philadelphia, 1980), pp. 21-50, regards the arrangement made in Jerusalem as an example of the *societas* agreements of Roman Law. Whether this was so understood by James and Peter may be doubted but this makes no difference to the responsibility Paul felt to raise the collection.

3. It is of no importance whether chapters 8 and 9 of 2 Corinthians come from the same letter or from two different letters which have now been combined in our 2 Corinthians.

4. It is necessary to note here a divergence with Paul's farewell address to the Ephesian elders. In it he apparently does not allow that they may receive support since he sets out his own practice of not receiving support as an example to them (Acts 20.33-5). There is also a divergence with 1 Tim. 5.17 if this refers to financial support. In the Miletus address he also makes a claim which is not found in his letters that by his work he supported his associates as well as himself.

5. A *societas* arrangment could not have been entered into as soon as Paul had arrived in Philippi. Time would have been needed for the growth of the necessary trust between Paul and the Philippians.

6. See Ronald F. Hock, *The Social Context of Paul's Ministry: Tentmaking and Apostleship* (Fortress Press, Philadelphia, 1980), pp. 52-55.

7. Hock, op.cit., pp.20-25.
8. Hock, op.cit., p.25.
9. Cf. J. Murphy-O'Connor, *St. Paul's Corinth*, pp. 167- 170.
10. See Best, 'Paul's Apostolic Authority-?', *J.S.N.T* 27 (1986), pp. 3-25.
11. Cf. Gerd Theissen, *The Social Setting of Pauline Christianity*, p.39.
12. Cf. Hock, op.cit., pp.22f.
13. Cf. Sampley, op.cit., pp. 85f.
14. Theissen, op.cit. p.39.
15. Cf Furnish, *II Corinthians*, pp. 507-8.
16. See Rinaldo Fabris, 'Il lavoro nel metodo missionario e pastorale di Paolo' in *Testimonium Christi: scritti in onore di Jacques Dupont* (Paideia Editrice, Brescia, 1985), pp.177-192.

VI

MEETING OPPOSITION

We go a stage further in relation to authority when we ask what happens when it is disputed or rejected. There is no doubt that Paul ran into such trouble from time to time; all do who have to make authoritative decisions. How did Paul react when he found himself opposed? It is necessary to distinguish between opposition assailing the church from outside and opposition emerging within it. Paul expected opposition from outside in the form of persecution. There was nothing he could do to prevent it as long as he continued to preach. But how did he respond to opposition which appeared in the communities he founded? He apparently met opposition in Jerusalem but we do not need to consider that because it did not come from his own converts.

Although Paul's converts criticised him we do not normally find them opposing him except when they have been upset by intruders from other Christian communities. Paul then normally opposes the intruders rather than his converts. We have no record of a personal encounter with these intruders. It is true he met opponents face to face in Jerusalem and Antioch (Acts 15.1-29) but neither were communities he had founded. Some had come to Antioch from Jerusalem arguing for the circumcision of Gentile converts and Paul had opposed them. In consequence Paul and Barnabas travelled to Jerusalem. Acts 15.12 says they defended themselves there by saying that God had worked signs and wonders among the Gentiles through them (Act 15.12). If either Gal. 1.18-24 or 2.1-10 is a separate account of this meeting we learn no more of what Paul or his opponents said.

There are however two accounts of head-on collisions of Paul with others. We find the first in Gal. 2.11-14. Things had been going well in Antioch. Peter was present and had fallen in with Gentile Christian ways. Then some came from James in Jerusalem and told Peter that as one who had been born a Jew he ought not to be adopting Gentile ways. So he withdrew from table-fellowship with Gentile Christians. Worse, his example affected others with the result that Barnabas and almost all the other Jewish Christians also withdrew. A major split in the community resulted. Paul tells us he withstood Peter face to face but not precisely what he said, though what follows in 2.15-21 may well be its substance. Here he presents a theological justification for the rejection of circumcision and the Jewish law as necessary to salvation. Judging by what he writes elsewhere in this letter he will not have been softly spoken to Peter and Barnabas. What he said to those who came from James can only be imagined! No element of hesitation or doubt is discernible in his attitude; and if there is none here when he deals with a fellow apostle we need not expect to find any when he comes to deal with those who have intruded into and disrupted the churches of his foundation.

The second place where we may surmise a personal antagonistic encounter is alluded to in 2 Cor. 2.5-11. Here Paul tells of someone who had caused trouble. (This was probably not the man who had earlier committed incest, 1 Cor. 5.1). There had been some kind of dispute and Paul had been supported by most of the Corinthians. The latter had themselves punished the offender who had repented (2 Cor. 7.5-12 apparently refers to the same incident). Paul is ready to forgive the man and hopes the Corinthians will do the same. Unfortunately we do not know what the man's original offence was. He may have been preaching a false gospel or stubbornly unwilling to accept Paul's ruling on some matter of behaviour. Whatever it was Paul had been able to overcome his opposition.

Tolerance[1]

In order to understand how Paul encountered opposition we need to take account not only of the occasions where he met it head on but also of the many where he did not oppose those who differed from him. We need to note that not everyone Paul rebuked is to be classed among his opponents. He criticised those in Thessalonica who had ceased to work (2 Thess. 3.6-13); since these did not form a 'party' or 'group' with a settled policy (they had no slogan 'Christians should not work') they cannot be taken as opponents. The charismatics in Corinth whom he criticised for over-stressing the importance of glossolalia were not opponents. He was probably criticised by the Thessalonians because at times he appeared to be no better than one of those travelling teachers or philosophers who lived off those whom they taught (1 Thess. 2.1-12), but even in their criticism the Thessalonians were not opponents for they accepted his position and authority. The line between criticism and full opposition is not always easy to draw. Friends incited by opponents may criticise but that does not make them into opponents.

In Corinth there were rival groups (it probably goes too far to describe them as 'parties') which formed themselves around the names of leaders, Paul himself, Peter, Apollos, and, strangely, Christ (1 Cor. 1.12). Presumably those in the groups other than the one which professed loyalty to Paul were to some extent opposing him (cf. 4.3-5). He for his part refused to have any quarrel with the followers of Apollos even though they may have fought with the group claiming to belong to Paul. 'I planted, Apollos watered' he says; both were part of the process by which God made the church grow (3.6). Paul then refused here to see or acknowledge opposition when it was possibly intended. Since he does not mention Peter in the same friendly way as Apollos it may be that he could not dispose so easily of the opposition of the Peter-group. Later in the letter he defends his position as an apostle claiming an equality in apostleship with Peter (9.1-7). We may deduce that in some way the followers of Peter (there is no reason to suppose Peter himself was personally involved) had attacked Paul's position. Despite their opposition Paul does not denounce them. He is content to stake out his own claim as an apostle and leave it at that.

Paul's polemic in 1 Corinthians 1-4 is then directed against the members of the fourth group, the so-called 'Christ-party'. They had emphasised wisdom and knowledge. In responding to their implied opposition Paul attempts to disarm them by asserting that he does not expect any group to use his own name. He reminds them that in Corinth he had only baptised a few of their number, that he had not been crucified for them and that none of them had been baptised into his name (1.12-16). There is thus no need for a Paul-group to exist and if no need for a Paul-group there is no need for any other, least of all for one which put central something Paul would never have put central, viz., wisdom and knowledge. The gospel's true centre is the cross and it does not easily harmonise with a message which depends for its success either on elequent presentation or on coming to terms with Greek philososphical thought or gnostic speculation. Yet while Paul implies that the the members of this group are unspiritual he does not deny they are Christians. They have been building up the church with wood, hay or straw while he and Apollos have used gold, silver and precious stones (3.10-15). He appeals to them to remember their oneness with other Christians in the church which is the temple of God (3.16). To some extent he also threatens them, saying that he will come among them as a father if necessary to discipline them (4.14-21). Paul, then, nowhere denounces this group with the vehemence with which he denounces the preachers of a false gospel in Galatia or those who entered the Corinthian community from outside and upset his work (see 2 Corinthians chapters 10-13). The Corinthian believers who have gone astray after wisdom are still his children in the faith and are to be treated as such and not as opponents. A phrase he uses in the discussion, 'when slandered, we try to conciliate'(4.13), aptly represents how he himself behaved in this matter.

Another division in the Corinthian community arose over food sacrificed to idols (1 Cor. 8.1-13; 10.1-30). Some refused to eat such food because they still partly feared the pagan gods whom the idols represented. Others, like Paul, ate because they had no such fears; the gods or their idols had no real existence and could not influence human affairs. Eating was therefore unable to harm anyone. Paul counsels the two groups to accommodate themselves to one another and bear with one another. He makes it clear that if he were living with those who had doubts he would respect their position and go along with them in refusing to eat: 'if food is a cause of my brother's falling, I will never eat meat, lest I cause my brother to fall' (8.13). Paul thus tolerates these people, though a neutral observer might be inclined to say that those who refused to eat were in fact acting as if they believed salvation came partly through that and not entirely through faith in Christ.

In Philippians we read of those who proclaimed Christ 'out of partisanship, not sincerely but thinking to afflict me (i.e. Paul) in my imprisonment' (1.17). Paul does not deny that these people preach Christ (if they had not done so he would have criticised them on that account) but suggests that they did so to trouble him by increasing the rigours of his imprisonment. It is difficult for us to understand how their preaching should do this and yet the preaching of those who preached out of genuine love should not affect him. We do not need to solve this problem. What interests us is Paul's attitude to them. He does not denounce them; he rejoices that whatever their motives Christ is preached. In showing tolerance towards those who had scruples over food sacrificed to idols and in not rejecting those who placed too high a value on wisdom Paul is dealing with his own converts, people whom he knows. He also knows those who had been preaching to add to his affliction in prison, though they may not have been his converts. We cannot determine who these people were for we cannot even be sure where Paul was held prisoner at this stage. What is important is that he is willing to tolerate those whom he personally knows even when he does not entirely agree with them.

The practice of tolerance which Paul displays in these passages he raises to a principle in Romans.[2] There again he deals with a division in the community over the eating of certain foods, a division compounded by a parallel one over whether certain days should be regarded as holy (14.1-15.13). He invites the rival groups to 'welcome one another, therefore, as Christ has welcomed you, for the glory of God'(15.7). He views the problem basically not as one about food and days but as one about how we should treat those with whom we disagree. Are the Roman Christians ready to accept as fellow Christians those with whom they are at variance in what is a matter of concern to them? Paul does not plea for an attitude of indifference-'it will all be the same in a hundred years'-but for a positive welcome for those with whom we do not see eye to eye. In Phil. 4.2-3 he goes beyond tolerance in asking that those who have fallen out with one another should be reconciled. When the Corinthians had displeased him he wrote a letter to reconcile them to himself (2 Cor. 7.8). It may be that what underlies Paul's tolerance is his view that all, even believers, are sinners. If we are such and if God accepts us ought we not to accept one another?

Paul's tolerance has limits as we see when he rejects those who preach a gospel other than his (Gal. 1.8-9). How does he treat those whom he finds it difficult to tolerate?

Paul's opponents

Much scholarly labor has been devoted to the identification of Paul's opponents, in particular those with whom he had to deal in Galatia, Corinth and Philippi.[3] They have been regarded variously as Judaisers, gnostics, spiritual enthusiasts, libertines. Identification is difficult because we possess only Paul's refutation of their views. He can leave a lot unsaid because his readers know his opponents. He himself may not have been accurately informed about them or fully understood their views. They for their part have left us no statement of what they believed. It is impossible then to draw an accurate picture of them. Fortunately we do not need to do this for we are primarily interested in the way Paul treats them, in the way he faces up to them, and not in their views.

If at times we have some difficulty in doing even this we have to confess that we have little or no idea what they thought of him and are reduced to making guesses from allusions in his letters. We can assume that his opponents views would have been much more extreme than those of his converts. The latter must at times have reacted against his paternalism for he finds it necessary to refute the assertion that he lords it over their faith (2 Cor. 1.24). Yet he does not appear to have treated them as harshly as his opponents treated them; the latter, he says, make slaves of them, prey on them, take advantage of them, put on airs and strike them in the face (2 Cor. 11.20). If they did this to his converts the imagination fails at the attempt to reconstruct what they would have done to Paul.

While we cannot detail the position of his opponents[4] it is important to note that they objected chiefly to his claim to be an apostle and to his gospel. Some of the criticisms of his converts are clearly linked to these issues. For example his refusal to accept maintenance leads to the accusation that he is not an apostle.[5] His opponents appear to have been as certain they were right as he was. This certainty would have derived in varying proportions from their wisdom and knowledge, their possession of the Spirit, their use of the Old Testament, their knowledge of the historical Jesus. Different opponents would have emphasised each of these differently. In turn they would have despised Paul for his lack of one or other of their supposed advantages.

Converts and intruders

As we have seen Paul acted tolerantly towards his converts and those whom he personally knew. Did he display the same tolerance towards those who came into his churches from outside and turned them against him? We look now at what happened when the churches of Galatia, Corinth and Philippi were penetrated by those unsympathetic to Paul. We commence with Galatia.

Here Paul regularly distinguishes between the local community and the intruders. He asks his converts 'Who has bewitched you?' (3.1). He speaks of those who unsettle them (5.12; cf 1.7-9; 6.12-13). The converts though they may have given too ready a hearing to the intruders have not wholly departed from Paul's gospel, otherwise he would not have written to them. He repeatedly calls them his brothers. Once he terms them his 'little children' (4.19). He is confident of their response (5.10). He encourages them to restore those who may have sinned (6.1); he would have had no time for such advice (cf. that of 6.6) if he had thought they had gone over to the intruders. Yet he is not unaware that his converts stand in real danger. He admits he is perplexed over their behaviour (4.20) and fears he has laboured over them in vain (4.11). They had begun well but are now finding things difficult (5.7). He asks if they are 'so foolish' that 'having begun with the Spirit' they are 'now ending with the flesh' (3.3). Paul is simultaneously confident of them and afraid they are in the process of slipping away.

We cannot easily draw a similar or indeed any conclusion in respect of the Philippians. If the letter we have is the letter as Paul sent it there is no doubt that he expects his converts to withstand the threats to their faith for he only devotes one chapter, the third, to arguing against his opponents; in the remainder no fears about the faith of the community appear. Many scholars, however, regard our letter as an amalgam of three separate letters to Philippi and identify the third chapter as one of them. By itself this chapter tells us very lttle about the Philippians, though in it he does call on them to imitate him (3.17), something he would hardly have done if he had been worried about their continuance in the faith. Most of those scholars who take chapter 3 to be a separate letter associate 4.1 with it. There Paul is certainly confident of the Philippians for he calls them his 'joy and crown'.

2 Corinthians chapters 10 - 13 is the place where opponents appear most clearly in the Corinthian correspondence. It is generally agreed that these chapters come from a different letter than the earlier chapters and were probably written after them.[6] The earlier chapters showed Paul on good terms with the Corinthians and confident of their Christian position. We can see this from his appeal to them for increased giving to the collection as well as with his pleasure in the way in which they have dealt with an offender (2.5-11; 7.5-12) by responding eagerly to a stern letter he had written. Yet there is no doubt that the first nine chapters contain indications that opponents already exist; since however the opponents are more clearly delineated and Paul's attitude made more precise in chapters 10-13 we shall concentrate our attention on the latter.

In the final four chapters the community is in danger of falling into the hands of intruders. Paul assures the Corinthians of his love for them (11.11) but worries about their love for him: 'If I love you the more, am I to be loved the less?' (12.15) In contrast with what we find in Philippians and Galatians he never calls the Corinthians his brothers in these chapters.[7] Some uncertainty can be detected in his approach: 'I wish you would bear with me in a little foolishness. Do bear with me!' (11.1). He fears that when he visits them he may not find them what he wishes (12.20) and will have to punish some of them (that is some of the Corinthians and not the intruders; 13.1-10). He summons them to examine themselves to see if they are holding to their faith (13.5). He ends by praying for their restoration (13.9; the RSV translation 'improvement' is a little weak here).[8] 12.11, 'I ought to have been commended by you', suggests his converts had not stood up for him in the way he expected them to do when he came under attack from the intruders.

In his speech to the Ephesian elders Paul as pictured by Luke affirms his innocence. Judging however by his defence whatever attack there may have been came from a different quarter than any we have been encountering in the letters. He no longer refutes alleged failures in his character (e.g. changing his mind too easily, appropriating money falsely) or in his apostleship but testifies that if any of his hearers do not attain salvation the fault is not his (Acts 20.26); he had never failed to declare to them the complete gospel (20.27; cf v.20).

Self-defence

If opponents have called in question Paul's gospel and his apostleship, how does he defend himself?

In Galatians he commences with a historical account in which he asserts that it was God who called him to be an apostle and that this had been recognised by the leaders in Jerusalem for they had not limited or confined his gospel in any way (1.1 - 2.10). After this historical opening he moves directly to argue the truth of his gospel as soundly based on the Old Testament. This was an important point since his opponents had apparently used the Old Testament as the foundation for their claim that all believers should adhere to the Jewish Law. Paul reminds the Galatians that his own gospel had brought them freedom from the superstitious forces which had bound them in their pagan days and led them into a salvation which depended on faith. (The manner in which Paul argues at times from the Old Testament may not be our way but it was a way which was acceptable in the ancient world. He uses it because his converts have been led astray by what he regarded as an unscrupulous, though also skillful, use of the Old Testament by his opponents.)

Paul responds differently to the attack on his apostleship in 2 Corinthians 10-13, probably because the nature of the attack differed. He no longer traces his appointment back to God's call (perhaps he can assume they know this since he had made it clear in 1 Cor. 9.1-2; 15.8-10). Instead he argues that while he had been among them he had displayed the 'signs and wonders and mighty works' expected of an apostle (12.12). He explains why though an apostle he had not exercised the right of an apostle to maintenance (11.7-11; 12.14-18).[9] Perhaps because some attack had been made on a suspected antipathy to Judaism on his part he supplies the facts about his Jewishness (11.22). This is a point he argues in stronger terms in Phil. 3.5-6. To the Corinthians he is also careful to rebut slanders on his character. We do not know what these slanders were; they may have related to his handling of money, to his failure to visit them when he had promised to do so, or to any one of the thousand dirty tricks with which politicians, and unfortunately sometimes religious leaders, are accustomed to accuse one another. Finally, giving a long list of his trials (11.23-33; cf Gal. 6.17), he attempts to establish the genuine nature of his care for them. To summarise: Paul in his self-defence attempts to set straight the factual record, to defend himself from scurrilous slanders, and to demonstrate that the gospel he preaches is in accord with God's will.

117

He realises that at times he goes further than he should, especially in respect of his own character and achievements. He is forced by his opponents into self-commendation and boasting. When he does so he describes himself as speaking like a fool or a madman (2 Cor. 11.21, 23; 12.11). True boasting should not be about oneself but about the Lord (1 Cor. 1.31; Gal. 6.14). Even boasting about oneself, if there is to be such, must have limits (2 Cor. 10.13). We can understand Paul's reluctance to boast since undue boasting was widely reprobated in the ancient world.[10] It was however recognised that there were times when the truth about oneself must be told, in particular when defending oneself against charges, which is what Paul is doing in 2 Corinthians. It was also not regarded as a fault to point out what one had suffered in remaining true to one's way of life, as Paul does in 2 Cor. 11.23-33. It is indeed difficult to see how false accusations can be refuted without some explanation of one's conduct which might sound like boasting. We may in fact be glad that Paul was forced to boast for if he had not done so there are things about him we would never have known.

Paul's self-defence is much briefer in Philippians than in either of the two other letters. He points out his Jewishness but says that it gave him no priviliged position before God (3.3-11). Whatever value he once attributed to it he now rejects, yet he makes no claim to have attained all that God has designed for those who trust him (3.12-16).

Attack

Attack is said to be the best form of defence and Paul was not slow to carry the war into the enemy's camp. He does this in two ways. He shows how inadequate are the views of his opponents and he assails their sincerity and genuineness. Neither Philippians 3 nor 2 Corinthians 10-13 offer much in the way of solid argument refuting the theologies of those who oppose him. There is however considerably more in Galatians where quoting the Old Testament he shows the implications of their attempt to persuade the Galatians to accept some of the provisions of the Law: 'Cursed be every one who does not abide by all things written in the book of the law, and do them' (3.10). In the nature of the case it is however difficult to distinguish Paul's positive expression of his own views from his attack on those of his opponents. The two are inextricably interwoven. We should note however that he does not seek to blind his converts with a superfluity of words covering up deficiencies in his argument.

It is when he attacks the character of his opponents that he seems to go too far, especially when we relate this to the absence in Philippians and 2 Corinthians of a reasoned criticism of their views . He not only attacks his opponents directly but when he defends his own behaviour by listing what he has suffered in Christ's service he implies their relative failure. Positively he speaks of them as using magic to attain their ends (Gal. 3.1) and as maintaining their point of view only to evade persecution (Gal. 6.12). He is certain that if they continue to adhere to their false views they will fall under a curse (Gal. 1.8-9) and never be accepted by God. Those who have upset the Philippian church are dogs, evil-workers, mutilators of the flesh (3.2); their god is their belly (3.19; probably a reference to either gluttony or sexual lust); they are the enemies of the cross (3.18). Those who have troubled the Corinthians are 'false apostles, deceitful workmen, disguising themselves as apostles of Christ. And no wonder for even Satan disguises himself as an angel of light' (2 Cor. 11.13-14). They lead the Corinthians astray as the serpent led Eve astray (2 Cor. 11.3). This does not seem to us the proper language for Christian debate, although too often Christian discussion has degenerated into a slanging match. What are we to say when we find Paul using it?

No one would denounce others in the way Paul does unless they were extremely confident of their own correctness. Paul, apparently, had no doubts about himself, his confidence being based on his experience on the road to Damascus. Since that time he believed himself close to Christ and able to speak in his name. As we have seen he regularly spoke in this way to his converts[11] and there is no reason to suppose his confidence evaporated when faced with opposition.

If Paul spoke so harshly of his opponents did he regard them as within or outwith the church? Some of what he says appears to imply the latter. For the early Christians the church was the sphere of Christ; all else was the realm of the devil. If people are described as servants of Satan (2 Cor. 11.14) does this not then imply that they are outside the church? When the incestuous believer of 1 Cor. 5.1-5 is delivered to Satan this is done so 'that his spirit may be saved in the day of the Lord Jesus'. 1 Tim. 1.20 may not be by Paul but it shows us what was believed at that time. There two men are delivered to Satan not 'so that others may learn not to blaspheme' but 'that they may learn not to blaspheme'. Deliverance to Satan is not then necessarily abandonment in hell. When Peter rebuked Jesus about his need to suffer Jesus said to him 'Get behind me, Satan!'(Mark 8.33), yet Peter was not damned but continued as a disciple. (Many of our ideas of Satan are more influenced by Milton's *Paradise Lost* than by New Testament thought.) For Paul then to ascribe Satanic influence to his opponents may not be quite as harsh as it seems. The same conclusion emerges in another way. When Paul compares himself with the intruders in Corinth he asks 'Are they servants of Christ?' and replies that he is a better one (2 Cor. 11.23). He does not then deny that they serve Christ. He also speaks of the same people as 'false brothers' (11.26; cf. Gal. 2.4). If we stress 'brothers' here rather than 'false' it implies they are still within the church.

Paul's model

Under what model or role does Paul see himself as operating when he attacks his opponents? At first sight it might seem as if we should envisage him as fighting against them and thus as fulfilling a warrior role.[12] Paul does envisage himself in this way regularly but when he does so it is in the course of a war against the powers of evil outside the church. What he writes in 1 Thess. 5.8 in describing the weapons and armor of the Christian can be applied to himself (cf Phil. 1.29-30; 2.25; Philm v.2). In 1 Thess. 2.1-2 he writes of his fight to proclaim the gospel in Thessalonica. Only in 2 Cor. 10.3-5 does he use the image of struggle in relation to other Christians and there he writes not of attacking them but their arguments. The role of warrior or soldier is not then one he adopts when dealing with either his converts or his opponents.

What role does Paul then play when attacking those who have infiltrated his churches? It is again that of the parent. This appears explicitly in 2 Cor. 12.14 in the middle of his onslaught on them; here he defends himself for his refusal to accept financial support from the Corinthians: 'I seek not what is yours but you; for children ought not to lay up for parents, but parents for children' (cf. Gal. 4.19). As founding father of his churches he has rights within them and he expresses his astonishment that the Galatians so quickly desert 'him who called' them to the grace of Christ (1.6). Parents normally protect their children from outside forces which would disrupt the home; the virulence of Paul's defence of his converts resembles nothing less than that of parents who see their children threatened. Like a good parent he is willing to perish so that his children may live (Rom. 9.3; cf. 1 Cor. 9.27).

Conclusions

Paul's real concern is for his converts and he will defend them under all circumstances. He treats them in a different way from that in which he treats intruders. He permits a wide variation of theological opinion among them. Since the views of his opponents are not known to us with suffcient accuracy it is impossible to tell if they lay within the same broad spectrum. It would be easy to say that since Paul attacks them their views must have been heretical. Such an assertion would not allow for the considerable variety of theological view which scholars now believe existed in the primitive Christian community.[13] We do not know if the views Paul attacked are in fact found in other writers within the canon; we do not even know if Paul would have accepted all the writings in the canon. Before we rush to answer we should remember the difficulty that Luther had with more than one of the New Testament writings.

More worrying, however, is the way Paul denounces his opponents. He never indicates that he would like to talk things over with them. Whereas he reasons with his converts he attacks his opponents. He does not show the latter the same tolerance he displays to the former. He does not want to hear his opponents' point of view; they stand outside the pale and there is apparently no hope for them. They are servants of Satan (2 Cor. 11.13-14); Satan has not yet gained control over his converts (2 Cor. 2.11). We do not need to pursue this further since our main theme is the relation between Paul and his converts. In any case we lack suffcient evidence to do so. It is important however that we note the differing attitude he adopts to those who have intruded, whom we might well have classified as Christian, from the protective attitude he shows to his converts.

Paul was personally acquainted with his converts but not so far as we know with those who intruded into his churches and disturbed them. Many of us are ready to pardon in those we know what we are not ready to pardon in those we do not know. We believe evil more quickly of those with whom we have no contact than of those we have. Because Protestants and

Catholics in N. Ireland have little personal contact they believe quite extraordinary things about one another. Paul having heard that some whom he had never met were disturbing his churches may see them in a much worse light than if he had been personally acquainted with them. It is relevant also to note that the Corinthians observed that while Paul could write tough letters when he was away from them when he was present his toughness seemed to disappear (2 Cor. 10.10). The Corinthians may here be misinterpreting a phenomenon many of us find in ourselves. We are angry when we hear of someone who has done wrong and we resolve to tell them off whenever we meet them but when we actually encounter them we draw back from expressing our anger. As we look at them our feelings change and we make allowances for them in a way we never did in their absence. If Paul had met his adversaries face to face then though his letters against them were tough his words and attitudes toward them might have changed.

Notes

1. See P. Richardson, *Paul's Ethic of Freedom*, Westminster, Philadelphia, 1979, passim.

2. Cf R. Jewett, *Christian Tolerance: Paul's Message to the Modern Church*, Westminster, Philadelphia, 1982.

3. No opponents had inflitrated the Thessalonian church, see Best, *1 and 2 Thessalonians*, pp. 16-22.

4. 'Mirror-reading', i.e. the deduction of the views of opponents from the statments of an author, is a hazardous process; see Lyons, op.cit.

5. See above pp. 99f.

6. While earlier opinion took these chapters to precede chapters 1-9 they are now generally held to be later; cf. C.K. Barrett, *The Second Epistle to the Corinthians*, A. & C. Black, London, 1973, pp.243-4; F.F. Bruce, *I & II Corinthians* (New Century Bible), Eerdmans, Grand Rapids, 1980, pp. 166-170; Furnish, *II Corinthians*, pp.37-8; R.P.Martin, *2 Corinthians* (Word Biblical Commentary), Word Books, Waco, 1986, pp. xlvi-li.

7. 13.11 is an exception but it is not clear if 13.11-14 is the original ending to the letter of chapters 10-13. Even if it is whoever brought the letters together may have edited it to produce a friendly conclusion.

8. N.E.B. 'all may be put right'; G.N.B. 'that you will become perfect'.
9. See pp. 99-105
10. Cf. Plutarch, 'On praising oneself inoffensively', *Moralia* 539A - 547F and Lyons, op.cit. pp.53-9.
11. See above pp. 81-5
12. On Paul's view of himself as one engaged in a struggle see V.C. Pfitzner, *Paul and the Agon Motif* (Supplements to Novum Testamentum xvi), Brill, Leiden, 1967.
13. See J.D.G. Dunn, *Unity and Diversity in the New Testament*, S.C.M., London, 1977.

VII

SHARING TOGETHER

We turn now to the second of the two main types of model which controlled Paul's relations with his converts: the reciprocal. It appears most obviously in the metaphor of the body, though Paul never explicitly connects his pastoral attitudes to it. He never says: 'I am a member of the body like the rest of you.' The model however underlies many of the ways in which he treats his churches. We need do no more than briefly indicate the theological significance that Paul put into the phrase 'the Body of Christ'[1] since we are primarily concerned with its practical interpretation. He employs it to relate believers to one another and as a group to Christ but not to describe the purpose of the church in the world (believers as Christ's hands and feet doing his work). He never points to any particular member of the body and says that that member possesses authority. When in Colossians and Ephesians the head is picked out the head is not some ecclesiastical official but Christ. All others, leaders and led, ministers and laity, remain on the same level; it truly defines a reciprocal relationship. All within the Body have at least one common task-to build one another up. Spiritual gifts are to be used for this purpose (1 Cor. 14.5,12). Paul himself labours to build up others and is not alone in this (1 Cor. 3.10-15). Mutual building up is the duty of church members (1 Thess. 5.11; Rom. 15.2)

Such a relationship implies a basic equality for all within it. There are other areas in which Paul's thinking is founded on equality. All are sinners. All are justified by the same grace of God in Christ. All are engaged in the same conflict (Phil. 1.29-30). In Christ humanity is not divided up into male and female, slave and free, Jew and Gentile. No special position is given in the church to those with wealth, learning or moral achievement.

The interchange of life

Though the model of the body does not appear in the brief letter to Philemon that letter provides a good jumping-off place for our discussion. Paul says that he has derived much joy and comfort from Philemon's love because the hearts of the saints have been refreshed through him (v.7). His own heart will have been among those refreshed (cf. v. 20). An almost identical phrase crops up in 1 Cor. 16.18 where Paul says that when Stephanas and others came to him from Corinth they 'refreshed my spirit' (cf. 2 Cor. 7.13 where RSV 'set at rest' is from the same Greek root). Although Paul never applies the word to his own activity we can be sure that he would have regarded his pastoral work as a 'refreshing' of his converts. We thus have a fully reciprocal relationship.

At first sight this may appear to be a perfectly normal human experience lacking any special Christian flavor: any person can refresh another. That there is something deeper in what Paul says is suggested by the words 'in Christ', 'refresh my heart in Christ' (Philm 20). As Paul uses the phrase 'in Christ' and allied phrases ('in the Lord', 'in Christ Jesus', etc.) they are often linked to the concept of the Body of Christ in that they relate Christians to one another. Paul sometimes uses them in a way which gives him a position of superiority (cf. 1 Thess. 4.1; 2 Cor. 2.17; 12.19); Timothy is Paul's child in the Lord (1 Cor. 4.17). But he also uses them without this sense of superiority. He has fellow-workers in Christ (Rom. 16.3,9). If widows re-marry they are advised to do so 'in the Lord' i.e. within the bounds of the church (1 Cor. 7.39). Paul and his converts are together 'one body in Christ' (Rom. 12.5). Paul instructs the Roman Christians to receive Phoebe 'in the Lord' (Rom. 16.2) which does not simply mean to receive her in a Christian manner or because she is a Christian; the phrase is used because both she and they are together in Christ, fellow-members of the Body. So when Paul bids Philemon refresh him in Christ he is not merely saying 'refresh me in a Christian way' but 'refresh me because both of us are Christians and there is a special refreshment which belongs to Christians'.

2 Cor. 1.3-7 is one of the most remarkable passages in Paul's letters concerning his relationship with his converts. In it he says he has suffered, though he does not say when or in what way he suffered. He is not referring to the kind of suffering which may come to anyone through a serious illness, anxiety over a loved one, or a natural disaster. Whatever the nature of his suffering it had resulted from his Christian activity and would never have taken place if he had not been a Christian. In his suffering God had comforted him (vv. 4-5). He does not enlarge on the nature of that comfort other than to imply it related to salvation. It was much more than a purification of his soul; his fellowship with Christ and his experience of salvation were deepened. That God comforted Paul does not surprise us; what does is that he goes on to say that the Corinthians also have been comforted through the comfort he received in his suffering. It is true that some of us are comforted and pleased when others suffer ('she got what was coming to her'). That is not what Paul has in mind. Nor is he suggesting that he will be good at comforting others because he himself has suffered. What he says is that he has been afflicted for their 'comfort and salvation' and comforted for their comfort (v.6). Paul's comfort has been transferred to the Corinthians. We are reminded of 1 Cor. 12.26 where in working out the image of the body Paul says that if one member suffers, all suffer together. In 2 Cor. 1.3-7 he has taken this a little further: if one member suffers and is comforted all are comforted (cf. 2.3, 'my joy [is] the joy of you all').

In a later passage (2 Cor. 4.8-12) in the same letter Paul returns to the theme of his suffering. He has been afflicted, perplexed, persecuted, struck down yet has been able to display the life of Jesus through it all. Then he concludes not as we might expect 'in the death that is at work in us as we suffer you can see the life of Jesus shining out to all the world' but 'so death is at work in us, but life in you'. Salvation is at work among the Corinthians beause he, Paul, suffers. This idea is familiar to us in relation to Christ and believers: Christ suffered, we live. Paul is not however putting himself on the same plane as Christ. He is very much aware that Christ died for all and that it was he and not Paul who was crucified for the Corinthians (1 Cor. 1.13). If indeed Christ had not first died for them then Paul's sufferings would never have brought life to them. The Body of Christ, the church, lives because Christ died and rose. Had he not done so the Body would not exist. But what holds for the existence of the Body holds also within it in a lesser way: death in one Christian may bring forth life in others.

Similar ideas are expressed, though not always as profoundly, in other passages. In 2 Cor. 7.3 Paul says to his readers 'you are in our hearts, to die together and to live together.' In 1 Thess. 2.8 he writes of his readiness to share with his converts not only his gospel but his very self. He tells the Philippians that he is ready to be poured out as a libation upon the sacrificial offering of their faith (2.17). When others suffer for the faith he is not a spectator; he suffers with them; so he ends the long list of his own sufferings for the gospel with the words 'Who is weak, and I am not weak? Who is made to fall, and I am not indignant (2 Cor. 11.29)?

But this is no one-way process with Paul always the giver. It is a reciprocal relation. Sometimes Paul is the recipient, though naturally there are fewer references in the letters to such occasions. To the Thessalonians he says 'we live, if you stand fast' (1 Thess. 3.8), and he does not mean he has more physical vitality if they successfully endure persecution, as if their example set the adrenalin flowing more strongly in his veins. The life to which he refers is the life of the Spirit belonging to the Body of Christ of which they are all members. It is then 'gospel', 'good news', to him when they stand firm and love (3.6).[2] When the Philippians send him money (4.15-17) to assist him in his work this is much more than money; it is their love flowing to him in the Body of Christ (cf Rom. 15.27). Their prayer helps toward his salvation (Phil. 1.19).[3]

When Paul is comforted by God that comfort is passed on to the Corinthians (2 Cor. 1.3-7); comfort can also flow in the opposite direction, from them to him. There had been trouble in Corinth over one person who had disturbed the church. After the trouble had been resolved Paul wrote to them 'I have great confidence in you; I have great pride in you; I am filled with comfort. With all our affliction, I am overjoyed' (2 Cor. 7.4). He ends his discussion of how they had behaved with 'therefore we are conforted' (7.13). So, as we have seen, Paul is 'refreshed' by them (Philm 7; 1 Cor. 16.18).

Partnership (koinōnia)
Paul writes of Philemon and himself as partners (v.17). He does not write 'I regard you as my partner' which might sound a little patronising but 'if you consider me your partner'. The context does not enable us to identify in what Paul and Philemon were partners but it will have been in some way in the work of the gospel. In his opening prayer in his letter to the Philippians Paul thanks God for their partnership in the gospel (1.5), presumably in its spread and preservation. The Philippians had also entered into partnership with Paul by sending him money for his later evangelisation in Thessalonica (4.15-16).[4]

Paul uses the language of fellowship or partnership more frequently in Philippians than in any other letter and Sampley [5] regards this as denoting the existence of a legal relation (*societas*) between the Philippians and himself. Consensual *societas* was in Sampley's words 'a prevalent partnership contract of Roman law, where each of the partners contributed something to the association with a view towards a shared goal.'[6] Such a legal relation was appropriate in the case of Philippi for it was a Roman foundation where Roman law was known and where Latin was the official language. *Koinōnia* is the Greek equivalent of *societas*. The essence of the relationship in this particular case was the financial support the Philippians gave to Paul as their missionary in areas beyond their own and Paul's willingness to be their missionary. Mutual trust with Paul had enabled them to enter into the relation. The relative absence of this term in connection with Paul's relationships with other churches may be occasioned because either they were not accustomed to Roman law or the necessary mutual trust did not exist.

Sampley of course never suggests that Paul came to this understanding of his relations with the Philippians through his familiarity with Roman law. Rather he uses the legal term to express an already existing mutual trust. If the underlying fellowship had not been there he could not have used the term. It enables him to say much the same as he says elsewhere using the body metaphor.

It would however be incorrect to view Paul's relations with the Philippians in terms of either a legal or financial arrangement: he engages in mission work; they send him contributions. Paul's partnership with the Philippians means that together they participate in the grace of God (cf. Philm 6 where Paul and Philemon share in the same faith) and it includes their mission activity in their own city (1.5,7). We move here again in the same area as in 2 Cor. 1.3-7.[7] Paul suffers as a prisoner[8] and the Philippians participate in his comfort. In their turn as they defend and confirm the gospel they bring him comfort and joy.

They have also taken a share in his troubles (4.14) by giving themselves and their money (4.15). Moreover wherever Paul is in prison his fellow-Christians are strengthened to speak the gospel without fear (1.14).

In other letters where Paul uses *koinōnia* it often implies a mutual sharing in something.[9] In 1 Cor. 9.23 Paul uses a compound of the root adding *sun*, 'with', indicating that he shares with others in the blessings of the gospel. When the word is used of the collection in 2 Cor. 8.4 ('taking part' in the RSV) it implies that two groups of people, givers and recipients, are brought together. In 1 Cor. 1.9 the meaning need not be restrictd to 'fellowship' with Christ but may include the fellowship of Christians with one another. This mutuality is probably also present in 1 Cor. 10.16 ('participation' in the RSV) because it leads on to a 'togetherness' in v.17.

Partnership can be expressed also through prayer. In Philemon we find Paul both praying for Philemon and asking for prayers for himself (vv. 4,22). In his longer letters Paul includes other and more detailed prayers. 1 Thess. 3.11-13 is typical:

> Now may our God and Father himself, and our Lord Jesus, direct our way to you; and may the Lord make you increase and abound in love to one another and to all men, as we do to you, so that he may establish your hearts unblamable in holiness before our God and Father, at the coming of our Lord Jesus with all his saints.

There are three requests here and these recur in other prayers: (i) that Paul may be able to visit them (cf 1 Thess. 3.10; Philm 22; Rom. 1.9-10); (ii) that they may grow in Christian virtue (cf Phil. 1.9-11; 1 Thess. 5.23; Rom. 15.13); (iii) that they may be saved at Christ's return (cf 1 Thess. 5.23; 1 Cor. 1.8; Phil. 1.9-11). We have no need to detail every request Paul offered for his converts. The regularity of his prayers demonstrates his care for them. It is a care which he expects to be returned in their prayers for him. The paraenetic sections of his letters contain many exhortations to prayer though not always

131

indicating their subject matter. From time to time however Paul instructs his readers to pray for himself. Aware that there are many dangers which still threaten him and his mission he urges the Corinthians: 'You also must help us by prayer, so that many will give thanks on our behalf for the blessing granted us in answer to many prayers' (2 Cor. 1.11). He seeks the prayers of the Philippians that the preaching which goes on while he is in prison may succeed and that he himself be able to continue to face with courage the trials of imprisonment (1.19-20; cf 2 Thess. 3.1-2). But just as some of his own prayers for others are in the most general of terms so are some of his requests for prayer for himself, e.g. 'Brethren, pray for us' (1 Thess. 5.25).

Brothers

When Paul terms his converts his brothers this indicates that he and they stand on the same level for by its very nature 'brother' is a reciprocal relation. The first Christians derived the term from Judaism but it was also one which Paul's Gentile converts could appreciate since it was in use in many contemporary cults. It serves to distinguish those within a community from those outside by creating a bond between those within. So Paul speaks of 'brotherly love' (1 Thess. 4.9; Rom. 12.10).

Many of the ways in which Paul uses 'brother' do not directly concern us, as when he speaks of the brothers of the Lord (Gal. 1.19), applies it to co-workers (1 Thess. 3.2; 1 Cor. 1.1; 16.12) or uses it as a description of the members of the church when it almost equals 'Christian' (1 Cor. 7.12,15; 16.20). However Paul frequently uses it in the vocative in addressing his converts. Here it is often found as part of stereotyped phrases: 'I want you to know, brethren,...' (1 Cor. 10.1; 2 Cor. 1.8; Gal. 1.11), 'I appeal to you, brethren,...'(1 Cor. 1.10; 1 Thess. 4.1,10). It is also used to introduce a new subject (1 Cor. 10.1; 12.1; 15.1), a fresh aspect of an existing subject (1 Cor. 2.1; 3.1; 14.26), to emphasise a conclusion (1 Cor. 4.6; 7.24; 14.39) or a particular statement (1 Cor. 14.20; 15.31). In none of these cases does its use appear significant.

This changes however when we see Paul employing it in places where its use is appropriate to its context. This is so when he uses it in relation to the way one convert should treat another where a word like 'Christian' would weaken the impact (1 Cor. 6.5-8; 8.11-13; 1 Thess. 4.6). Paul must then have seen it as an important word. It is appropriate to the discussion in 1 Cor. 1.11 where brothers are expected not to quarrel. It is appropriate when Paul wishes to show that his converts stand on the same level as himself. They should be not his babes but his brothers (1 Cor. 3.1; cf. 14.20). As his brothers they should become as he is (Gal. 4.12; cf Phil. 3.17; 1 Thess. 2.14; 1 Cor. 4.6). Paul labours and speaks in tongues as his brother converts do (1 Thess. 2.9; 1 Cor. 14.6,18). As a Jewish Christian he puts himself on the same level as his Gentile brothers (Gal. 4.28). He calls his converts his brothers when in some way he wishes to show his close relation to them: when he misses their presence (1 Thess. 2.17), is comforted to learn of their faith (1 Thess. 3.7), wants them to pray for him (1 Thess. 5.25).

It might seem that a tension would exist between Paul's description of himself as both parent and brother of his converts. However he derived these two descriptions from two different metaphorical fields and in consequence was probably not fully aware of their possible inconsistency. In 1 Cor. 14.20 he tells his brothers to mature where we might have expected him to refer to them as his children (cf. 2 Thess. 3.6). The two metaphors intermingle in 1 Thess. 2.7-11. Metaphors never express more than a part of the truth and possess only a limited area of appropriateness beyond which they should not be extended. They serve to bring out certain truths and must not be pushed beyond these truths. Parent and brother typify the

133

twofold relation Paul had with his converts. His parenthood was a historical fact which could never disappear. His brotherhood was something he wished to develop until it became the principal relation. So he regrets that he has to treat his brothers as babes (1 Cor. 3.1).

If Paul did not fully resolve the tension between his roles as parent and sibling neither did he explore how the latter relation within the religious activity of the church should work itself out in economic and social affairs. Christians are still trying to do this.[10]

In Gal. 4.12-20, a passage which commences 'Brothers', there is a string of statements which do not appear to cohere. It may be that Paul was emotionally agitated at this point because of his relations with the Galatians. H.D. Betz [11] suggests however that he uses here a *topos* or theme frequent in ancient literature, that of friendship. The theme (it may reappear in 2 Cor. 7.3[12]) and the recognized marks of true and false friendship may be assumed as known to the Galatians and Paul can therefore play on their knowledge. For the contemporary world true friendship was possible only among equals. If this is the correct understanding of the passage it provides another instance of a reciprocal relation between Paul and his converts.

It might seem that some light would be thrown on that reciprocal relation through Paul's use of the first person plural. Mostly his letter alternate between 'I' (or a 'we' which means 'I' or represents Paul and his co-workers) and 'you'. When Paul uses 'we' with the intention of including his readers it is generally in statements which are universally true ('food will not commend us to God', 1 Cor. 8.8) or statements of a confessional nature ('for our sake he made him to be sin who knew no sin', 2 Cor. 5.21; cf 1 Cor. 15.3; Gal. 1.4). At the level of faith and belief Paul and his converts stand on the same plane. In some respects they also stand on the same plane in regard to missionary activity: they are engaged in the same conflict (Phil. 1.30); they are examples to others as he was to them (1 Thess. 1.7); they are missionaries as he was (1 Thess. 1.8). When however it comes to instruction and rebuke Paul is on a different level.

Slaves and servants

These are two terms which Paul uses of himself and others which might be regarded either as denoting reciprocal roles or superior/inferior roles. In the latter case Paul is in the inferior position. English translations of these terms often vary and 'slave' (*doulos*) is rendered 'servant' and 'servant' (*diakonos*) rendered 'minister'. There are similar variations in the verbal forms.

Paul uses the term 'slave' of actual slavery and then metaphorically of enslavement to sin or to pagan gods (e.g. Rom. 6.6, 16-20; Gal. 4.3-9). Jesus is said to take the form of a slave though he never actually was a slave (Phil. 2.7). The word serves to denote the lowliness of his earthly position in comparison both with his pre-incarnate state and that of other human beings (Mark 10.44). Paul uses the word in relation to his own position and that of others over against God (e.g. Rom. 6.22; 7.25) and Christ (e.g. Rom. 1.1; Gal. 1.10). It does not necessarily denote lowliness.[13] Members of the Roman bureauocracy could be termed slaves, as were Moses, David and the prophets (e.g. 2 Kings 18.12; 2 Sam. 7.5; Jer. 7.25). To call oneself a slave or servant of God does not however relate one to others. Paul however also uses it in this way and terms himself 'a slave to all' (1 Cor. 9.19). He is the slave of those to whom he preaches (2 Cor. 4.5). Since he also tells the Galatians to be 'slaves of one another' (5.13) the term denotes a reciprocal role. Used in this way any idea of superiority is removed and Jesus can be seen to be the model. If 'superiority' is indeed intended then Paul's converts are the superiors.

The same is true in general of Paul's use of 'servant' ('minister'). This term is employed in the Gospels to describe

Christ's ministry to us (Mark 10.45) and Paul employs it in the same way (Rom. 15.8). However he uses it more frequently of his ministry to his converts (2 Cor. 5.18; 11.8; 1 Cor. 3.5). Because that ministry is also his ministry to God it is often difficult in particular texts to distinguish which aspect is uppermost in his thought (2 Cor. 4.1; 6.3). Paul also uses the term of the ministry of Christians to one another (1 Cor. 12.5; 16.15; Rom. 12.7; 16.1). In particular he applies it to the sending of the collection to Jerusalem (Rom. 15.25; 2 Cor. 8.4,19,20, etc.). Since he uses it extensively in 2 Corinthians it may have been a word whose use the Corinthians had developed. If so Paul refuses to allow them to restrict it to themselves or those who were opposing him and applies it to himself: 'Are they servants of Christ? I am a better one'(2 Cor. 11.23). He then proceeds to recount all that he has suffered in the cause of the gospel. If he has any superiority it lies not in being given honour but in suffering. As Paul uses the term then it is basically reciprocal and with 'slave' it is appropriate at this point in our discussion.

Notes

1. I have discussed this at length in my book *One Body in Christ* (S.P.C.K., London, 1955); for a more recent treatment see R. Banks, *Paul's Idea of Community*, pp. 62-70.

2. Cf my *I & II Thessalonians*, pp.138-45.

3. Cf. F.W. Beare, *The Epistle to the Philippians*, A & C Black, London, 1959, p.62.

4. See p. 100

5. *Pauline Partnership in Christ*, pp. 51-78.

6. Op.cit., p.11.

7. J. Hainz, *KOINONIA* (Biblische Untersuchungen 16), Verlag Fredrich Pustet, Regensburg, 1982, p. 102.

8. It is irrelevant to our purposes whether Paul was a prisoner in Rome, Ephesus or Caesarea.

9. On *koinōnia* generally see also G. Panikulam, *Koinōnia in the New Testament: A Dynamic Expression of Christian Life* (Analecta Biblica 85), Rome, Biblical Institute Press, 1979; M. McDermott, 'The Biblical

Doctrine of *KOINONIA*', *Biblische Zeitschrift*' (1984), pp. 64-77, 219-233.

10. Petersen, op.cit., pp.97-8.

11. *Galatians* (Hermeneia), Fortress, Philadelphia, 1979, pp. 220-37.

12. Cf. Furnish, *II Corinthians*, pp. 367, 370-1.

13. Cf. R. Jewett, 'Romans as an Ambassadorial Letter', *Interpretation*, 36 (1982), pp.5-20.

VIII

CONCLUSIONS

It is important now to draw together what we have been doing and attempt to assess it.

A clash of roles?

We have seen that Paul viewed his activities under a number of different models. Are these compatible? If they are not any incompatibility will obviously lie between the superior/inferior roles and the reciprocal roles.[1] Before we over hastily reprobate an incompatibility we should remember that we all operate with several models of behaviour in our daily lives. The teacher/student relationship which is basically one of superiority and inferiority changes when teacher and student are members of the same team in a sports contest into a reciprocal relationship, returning to the former when the class room is re-entered. In the case of Paul the superior/inferior relation issues out of his activity as founder of his churches. When he went to a new city and preached he was the 'expert' in Christian living and thinking and so necessarily the superior. The reciprocal relation however comes from his theology of the church. (When he lists the roles which arise out of his view of the church in 1 Cor. 12.28 and Rom. 12.6-8 he does not include the parental.) Yet both relations connect up with his love for his converts as we have already seen in relation to the parental role.[2] When we examine his principal description of the church as the Body of Christ (1 Cor. 12.12-31) and the duty of members in it, which includes his own duty, we note that he moves directly from it to the theme of love as governing all activity in the Body (chapter 13). Love is both the base from

139

which parenthood operates and the tie which binds together members of the Body in reciprocal action.

The course of church history might be described as in part the struggle between these two models, the superior/inferior and the reciprocal. The first tends to produce some form of hierarchical government within the church, the latter a charismatic. In practice a mixture of both exists in every church and both are probably necessary.

Leadership

We have not previously used the term 'leader' regularly[3] to characterise the superior/inferior relation since Paul himself does not use it but it could be a general term to signify his relation to his converts. There have been many studies of the nature of leadership.[4] Most relate to small groups and the emergence of leaders within them. They agree in showing that there are no inborn characteristics which ensure that certain people will end up in such positions. It is true that some leaders, as De Gaulle, have been of commanding physique but not all have and there is no reason to suppose Paul was. The Corinthians regarded his bodily presence as weak (2 Cor. 10.10).

The manner in which leadership operates in small groups lies closer to Paul's reciprocal models than his superior/inferior ones. Within small groups different people emerge as leaders in different areas of activity. The permanently structured superior/inferior relation is neither encouraged nor supposed to happen. Although Paul's churches were not large it is not easy to apply the small group concept to his leadership of them. He did not become leader of any of his churches in the way in which leaders normally appear in small groups. He founded the small group in each city. The very tiny nucleus which drew converts to itself consisted of Paul and whatever associates were with him. From the first day of the group's existence he was its leader. The little house groups which he left behind him when he went to a new city may after his departure have provided good examples of the emergence of leaders [5] according to the small group pattern but the church while he was present did not.

Paul's leadership[6] was not however confined to the individual churches he founded; he had also a position of leadership within the whole church. How did he come to that position? When he first became a Christian he joined an already existing group in Damascus. He did not join it as leader as if he had been sent down from headquarters staff in Jerusalem to take over a district branch. If in small groups leaders emerge in relation to restricted areas of activity Paul may quickly have become the leader in preaching in Damascus (Acts 9.20-22). It would have been no small feather in the cap of the local Christians if a prominent persecutor went to the synagogues and proclaimed the very gospel he had been sent to attack. The group may well have pushed him forward into this leadership role. If his leadership commenced in the area of speech it certainly continued to be effective in this area. With time it extended also into other areas of pastoral care and organisation. It must be emphasised that Paul himself would not have regarded our suggestion as a satisfactory description of the origin and development of his leadership. He would have attributed it to his experience on the Damascus road. Like his gospel, his leadership was given him by God, not man.

Paul would also have denied that he was the leader of his churches. The true leader was Jesus as Jesus also was the true founder. When then we speak of Paul as founder or leader we are speaking in sociological rather than theological terms. The Body of Christ may have come into existence in Corinth because Paul went there and preached and it would not have come into existence when it did if Paul had not gone to Corinth with the gospel, but the Body is the Body of *Christ* not of Paul.

Understood in that sense the type of leadership which Paul exercised related to a situation in which he was the historical founder of the groups he led. This kind of situation has not recurred often in the history of the church. Pastors in congregations are rarely founders. They may bring individuals into the group through conversion but the group existed before they ever came to be its pastor. This is true even of those who enter new housing areas to develop new churches for they commence with a nucleus of Christians from other congregations who have moved to the area and been persuaded to break their links with their former congregations. The normal pastor today is not then in Paul's position. The missionary pioneer has often been and we can find other parallels in church history.

Parallels are of course easier to come by in other spheres of activity, e.g. among those who have founded new industries. Characteristic of many of these has been a refusal to surrender the positions of leadership which they created for themselves. They have continued to keep a firm hand on all that went on within their 'empires'. The same has been true of a number of church leaders. It was almost inevitable in the case of William Booth because of the structure he gave to his creation, the Salvation Army. Hudson Taylor who founded the China Inland Mission maintained a firm control over all its activities until his death.[7] Founders of monastic orders tended to prescribe in great detail the course their members' lives should follow. If mission pioneers in the field have been sometimes loath to permit power to slip from their grasp into the hands of indigenous Christians they have not always been encouraged to do so by mission boards at home.

There is room to provide evidence from only one case, John Wesley. He left behind him in his Journal and letters a mass of material which permits his attitude to be well documented. He may have been different from Paul in that he worked among those who were nominally Christians rather than pagans yet there are many similarities with Paul. He founded a number of separate causes; he drew associates into his work; he revisited the groups he brought into existence and wrote extensively to them. He was in dispute with other Christians. He split with the Moravians largely over theological matters, over justifying grace and the law of God. A clash of personalities may have been part of the problem but ostensibly the split was on theology.

He wrote to some of his followers with whom he disagreed
I have borne with you long, hoping you would turn. But... nothing now remains, but that I should give you up to God. You that are of the same judgement, follow me.[8]

Here we see the same certainty in respect of the correctness of his own view as in Paul [9]. It was the same certainty about his theological position that led him to break with Whitfield over predestination, though here there was no personal animosity; they continued to meet, preached at one another's services and took part in the same love feasts. His rigidity however led some of his other earlier associates to break with him.

The structure which he provided to hold together the many causes he founded was based on himself[10]. He might be said to have been that structure. Some of his followers called him 'Pope John'[11]. Though he did call an annual conference into existence its function was not to govern but to advise[12]. It was not open to it to make majority democratic decisions[13]. He also exercised a strict control over his preachers[14]; they were his sons in the Gospel; he set down rules for their behaviour; they could not marry without his permission; he prescribed what they should read.[15]

His control extended to the different groups he had founded. When one Scottish associate allowed elders to operate in his society he wrote to him immediately to disband the group.[16] As for the individual members of classes or groups he knew many of them by name and could on occasion order their exclusion when their conduct displeased him.[17] When he revisited the classes he would personally examine the members to see if they were still worthy to belong.[18]

If Paul seems to us to be over-paternalistic in his dealings with his churches this is a trait which he shares with many who have founded new movements. The paternalistic imagery is not popular today yet other allied images are pervasive, e.g. the professional/lay or the expert/non-expert. There are those who 'know' and those who either are not thought worthy of knowledge or are carefully instructed in what they are allowed to know, often in condescending terms. Some scientists do not like moral judgements being passed on their work by non-scientests. Governments may conceal some of their activities from those who have elected them perhaps saying that the 'facts' are too complex for ordinary people to understand. This attitude is found even in the church. Only those who have been adequately trained in theology are capable of determining what the gospel is. Only those who have passed through some ceremony are able to provide spiritual sustenance for others. Only those who have had some special spiritual experience are able to know Jesus or bring others to him. If Paul cannot escape the accusation of paternalism he can that of being the 'expert'.[19] If ever he was such it was while he was a rabbi. When he became a Christian he rejected all his 'expertness' (Phil. 3.4-7; 'expertness' is 'confidence in the flesh'). He does not seem to care who baptises converts (1 Cor. 1.14-17) nor when he gave instructions about how the Eucharist should be celebrated does he say anything about who should preside at it (1 Cor. 11.17-34); we do not even know if he did so when he himself was present. He did not worry about the inner spiritual or moral condition of those who preached the gospel (Phil. 1.15-18).

Finally we should note that if Paul acted as leader he did not set up a subordinate system of local sub-leaders who would act below him mediating his instructions to his converts.[20] He was slow to delegate authority and did not create a hierarchy. (The only hierachy he recognised was that of God - Christ - man - woman; 1 Cor. 11.3). His associates, Timothy, Titus, Silvanus, whom he sent on missions to churches were personal assistants, not subordinate leaders in local churches. It is true that there were local leaders in the churches (1 Cor. 16.16; Phil. 1.1; 1 Thess. 5.12; in this last case the office does not even have a title nor are the leaders identified by name); these leaders probably emerged after he left. He may request his converts to acknowledge their position, to respect and obey them but it is noticeable that he does not normally call on these leaders to take action whenever problems arise in his churches. The one apparent exception is Phil 4.3 where he calls on his 'true yokefellow' to help in reconciling Euodia and Syntyche; the way however in which he appeals to this person does not suggest action in an official capacity. When he writes to churches he does not address their officials but each church as a whole. Again the one exception is Philippians (1.1) yet even here the bishops and deacons are brought in alongside the whole church and are never referred to again. When in 1 Cor. 3.5-6 he refers to leaders other than himself in order to prove that God uses many in his work he does not mention a local Corinthian but another missionary, Apollos. When he lists leaders in 1 Cor. 12.28 and Rom. 12.6-8 it is very difficult with the exception of apostles, prophets and teachers to pin down their exact position within the church, let alone within a church hierarchy. Those who view apostles as the crown of a hierarchy do so only because they view them not as local leaders but as universal.

Outside Paul's letters the case of the Ephesian elders may be adduced to show he set up a local leadership through which he acted (Acts 20.17-35; in 14.23 he is said to have appointed elders in various churches). Acts 20.17-35 is probably a Lukan construction. We have already noted a number of differences between the pastoral approach of Paul's speech and that of the letters.[21] These differences confirm the view of scholars that it does not reproduce one of his actual speeches. We note now that the term 'elder' never appears in any of the genuine letters. There is also a peculiarity about the summons to the elders to come to Miletus. This was a considerable distance from Ephesus. [22] Paul was in a hurry (v.16) yet he sent messengers to Ephesus to summon the elders to him. They would not have been able immediately to throw up whatever they were engaged in and journey to him. Their journey would have been slow since some of them would have been elderly. It would have been much easier for Paul to go to Ephesus and speak to them, or rather to the whole church.

We have to acknowledge then that though Paul desires his converts to behave in orderly fashion (1 Cor. 14.33,40) he did singularly little to organise them .[23] There is here a considerable difference from the attitude of Wesley. In the modern world we are accustomed when founding a new group to draw up a constitution for it and set up an administration within it. How else could it survive? Paul takes no steps to fulfil either of these ends. It may be said that he does not need to plan for the future since Christ will soon return. But even if we set up groups with a time limit on their activity we still give them an organisation. Paul leaves his converts free to work out their own organisation. But he does not leave them entirely free in this; they have the gifts of the Spirit. The situation as each church grows is fluid and it needs to work out for itself the way in which it would develop most satisfactorily. A firm line would have inhibited growth into maturity. Here Paul's leadership is not paternalistic but shows us another instance of his desire that his converts should mature.

Does Paul live up to his own standards?
It would not be proper to complete our discussion of Paul's

relationship to his converts without some attempt to evaluate it. But what should be our standards in doing this? It would be relatively easy to take some modern books on pastoral care and use them to assess his achievement. But such books are written in the light of our contemporary situation and employ present days theories of psychology. It would be unfair to judge Paul against standards of which he knew nothing. We must return to his own period and seek our yardstick there.

If we look to Paul's own time there are three possibilities. We might assess what he did by what people then regarded as good moral teaching, say that of the Stoics. Yet since Paul would have claimed that the values by which he lived derived not from Stoicism but from Jesus and Judaism this would again be unfair. We might then choose Jesus as standard. Paul could not complain since he both sets out Jesus as the perfect example of humanity (Phil. 2.5-11), who as the second Adam alone offered true obedience to God (Rom. 5.18,19), and attempts to imitate him (1 Cor. 11.1). It was into Christ's likeness that Paul was being changed (2 Cor. 3.18); it was to the image of God's son that he was being conformed (Rom. 8.29). These however are mainly theological statements and tell us little of the actual character and teaching of Jesus. Paul in fact reports nothing of the life of Jesus prior to his passion and relatively little of his teaching. Are we to judge him then on what we know of Jesus or on what we can be sure he knew? Since we cannot say with any certainty what Paul knew it would again be unfair to use this yardstick.

This leaves only one approach and it is the fairest: to evaluate Paul in terms of his own statements.[24] He was not slow to tell his converts how they should treat one another. Does he relate to them in the same way as he instructs them to relate to one another? We do not have far to go to look for his instructions to them. Most of these are fairly general as when he tells them to love one another (1 Thess. 4.9-12; Gal. 5.14). Gal. 6.1-2

147

however is more concrete and is a good place from which to begin since it deals with pastoral care:

> Brethren, if a man is overtaken in any trespass, you who are spiritual should restore him in a spirit of gentleness. Look to yourself, lest you too be tempted. Bear one another's burdens, and so fulfil the law of Christ.

It is fair to say that Paul did not lay his own burdens on others. Typical is his rejection of financial support. Equally there is no trace in his letters that he unloaded his spiritual and moral problems on them. He does not write to the Philippians: 'The Corinthians are giving me a perfectly miserable time; I don't know what to do.' It is also important to recognise that he helps his converts to bear their burdens. He does this every time he answers their queries about how to behave or what to believe. He does not exaggerate when he writes to the Corinthians of his anxiety for all the churches; when they are weak, he is weak with them (2 Cor. 11.28,29). We saw much of this when we examined his parental care for them.

But when his converts fail does he always restore them in a spirit of gentleness? It is more difficult to give a simple affirmative answer here. He is surely not responding in a spirit of gentleness when he is sarcastic (e.g. 1 Cor. 4.8),[25] when he threatens to come to the Corinthians and destroy rather than build up (2 Cor. 13.10), when he abuses those with whom he disagrees (Phil. 3.2; Gal. 5.12), when he consigns to hell those who preach another gospel (Gal. 1.8-9; certainly in this case he is not blessing in the way he advocates in 1 Cor. 4.12). Related to gentleness is tolerance and we have seen that Paul [26] both advocated and practised this. He was tolerant and conciliatory (1 Cor. 4.13) towards many of those with whom he disagreed but not always towards those who had intruded into what he claimed to be his territory and misled his converts.

Paul taught his converts to build one another up (1 Thess. 5.11), helping each other to mature. We looked earlier [27] at the way he himself assisted his converts to mature and saw that though he did much to achieve this end there were occasions when he was not as wholehearted as he might have been. He tells his converts to live at peace with one another (1 Thess. 5.13). The final four chapters of 2 Corinthians do not suggest that he always lived at peace with them, but then it takes two to make war and they had first broken the peace with him. We suggested earlier that in many of these cases when Paul seems to act unreasonably he was only following out the parental role where parents react more strongly than seems necessary when their children are attacked.

In Rom 12.10 Paul tells his readers to 'outdo one another in showing honour'. Did he seek honour for himself? If any honour belonged to being an apostle, and certainly some thought it did, Paul as we have seen only claimed to be an apostle when others forced him into it.[28] Except when as leader he directs their activity he does not appear to put himself on a higher plane than his associates. Silvanus and Timothy are apostles alongside him (1 Thess. 2.6). Apollos is classed on the same level as a co-worker in God's field (1 Cor. 3.5-9). Although he terms Timothy his child (Phil. 2.22; presumably because he was his convert) he can say that Timothy served (literally 'acted as a slave') alongside himself. Paul is happy at all times to be known as the servant or slave of Christ.[29]

In so far as Paul calls on his converts to imitate him[30] and he fails to reach his own highest standards there is an obvious problem. It is this very danger that inhibits preachers today in summoning their converts to imitate them. But as we have argued earlier if Paul did not set the pattern of his own life before his converts there was no other actual pattern he could set. To outline in words the behaviour of Jesus would not have provided an example sufficiently concrete for them to turn into action. In any case Jesus had lived in a different culture from Paul's converts and had never encountered many of their

149

problems. Paul had to translate both by precept and example the behaviour of Jesus into a new culture. If at times he failed we must recollect that he was not divine but human.

Part of our criticism of Paul is due to the two roles he plays, as parent and as fellow-Christian. We have used his statements about how his converts should treat one another, i.e. statements drawn from the reciprocal role, to examine his own behaviour when he plays the superior role. The difficulties to which we have pointed arise at least then in part from the necessity to play simultaneously two disparate roles. Some, but not all, of our criticisms may be discounted on this ground. But we cannot excuse in this way his sarcasm or his worry that his converts might put him to shame.

Paul's sensitivity

Closely related to all this is the question how sensitive Paul was to the needs and feelings of his converts. We may begin by substantiating a point made earlier when we suggested that there might be a difference in the way he wrote to the Romans who were not his converts from that in which he wrote to the churches which he himself had evangelised. In Romans he does not call on his readers to imitate him (he does imply imitation of Jesus in 15.1-3) for he realises they have never seen how he behaves. In Romans he avoids the parent/child imagery because his readers are not his children. Thus he does not use the type of argument which we saw him use in our discussion in Chapter II. He does not summon the Romans to obey him, but instead to obey Christ or the gospel (1.5; 2.8; 6.17; 10.16; 16.26). In other letters he recalls his readers to things he has previously taught them; he never does this in Romans. His use of the diatribe style of argument is almost exclusively restricted to Romans;[31] he has no need of an imaginary interlocutor in the other letters; he can argue directly with their readers. Romans offers a sustained discussion requiring no intimate knowledge of its readers; commentators have always had great difficulty in seeing how its paraenetic section tied in with the life of that church. When then Paul writes he is sensitive in respect of whether his readers know him or not. Apart from Romans this comes out in another way: as we saw in chapter VI he treats his converts differently from the way way he treats his opponents; the acerbity he shows to the latter is missing when he deals with those he knows.

He is sensitive in other ways. Whereas as a rabbi he must have had to study the Old Testament in Hebrew his quotations from it are almost invariably based on its Greek translation, the Septuagint. He never behaves like the preacher who says 'The English translation is not very good here; the Greek says ...' He accepts the translation his readers know and works within its terms. He does not feed his converts with 'meat' when 'milk' is their best nourishment. In the same way he picks up and uses illustrations from the world of his converts. Thus he uses athletic imagery to the Corinthians who know about the Isthmian games (1 Cor. 9.24-7) and he addresses the Thessalonians in the style of a Cynic-Stoic philosopher.[32] He is aware that the return of the converted Onesimus to Philemon will place the latter in a difficult situation; so he deals very tactfully with him, attempting to persuade where he might have commanded (vv. 8,9,14).[33] His tact is also apparent on many occasions, e.g. when he sees no reason for any group in Corinth to attach itself to his name (1 Cor. 1.13-15) or when he asks Philemon to consider him as his partner (v.17)[34].

It is to his sensitivity that we owe statements like those of 1 Cor. 9.19-23 and 10.33a where it is sometimes alleged that he behaves like a weather cock. If Paul appears unduly flexible on these occasions we must remember that he also knew how to stand firm (Gal. 2.11-14). His flexibility[35] is not that of the politician seeking votes but of one who is intent above all else in saving men and women (10.33b and note the constant refrain in

9.19-23). Sensitive to their thinking he will accept practices which, if left to himself, he would never have accepted.

It must be allowed there are also times when he appears insensitive to his readers. He can argue in an involved way and must on many occasions have lost his less well educated converts. They can hardly also have known their Bibles in the way he assumes, especially when his arguments depend on allusions to it. But what preacher has not failed in both these ways!

There is however a more serious point of insensitivity. Nowhere in his letters does he seem aware that others have been converted since he moved on from a particular church. New members must constantly have been added who would never have known him. His attitude to them would surely have differed from that to those whom he had converted. The new members could not be regarded as his children. He could not summon them to imitate him since they did not know his example. Yet he never writes 'As those who knew me will have told you' or 'newcomers will have heard of my way of life' or 'those of you who have joined since I left will have been told of my teaching on this point'. When he recalls his behaviour and teaching it is always in such a manner as to imply that all his readers have first-hand experience of them. It is not that he is unaware of changes in his churches; he knows of intruders who have come opposing him (2 Corinthians chaps 10-13) and of members who have failed (Gal. 1.6). Perhaps this insensitivity should be put down to a failure of imagination. It is again one to which we are all subject. We tend to take a static view of a situation we have left and assume that it will continue exactly the same until we return.

Pastor and theologian

Did Paul's pastoral practice accord with the basic tenets of his theology? Scholars have debated what the latter are and we shall not enter into that debate but take up a few of his ideas which would be accepted by all as in some way central to his thinking.

A reciprocal relationship requires an equality of those who share in it. That equality inheres deeply in Paul's theology. All are sinners and all are justified by the same grace of God in Christ. The equivalent of this in pastoral work would be the treatment of all in the same way, i.e. an acceptance of all without respect to external factors. Such factors would include those listed in Gal. 3.28 (Jew/Gentile, slave/free, male/female) as well as the areas of wealth, learning, and moral achievement. To put this another way: Was Paul as a pastor a respecter of persons?

So far as we can learn from his letters Paul made no distinction between Jew and Gentile. We find the principle guiding his practice in 1 Cor. 9.19-23. A large portion of his time was in fact taken up in a defence of the right of Gentiles to become Christians on the same terms as Jews and there is no point where we see him treating either group differently. Nor does he appear to have distinguished between slave and free. He had as close fellowship with and was as happy in the company of Onesimus as of Philemon. It is true that in the concluding greetings of his letters the rich and influential appear to be picked out for mention (e.g. 1 Cor. 16.15,19). This is natural since the Christian groups met in the houses of the more wealthy. To greet them would have been to greet all in the group. We cannot know if Paul when he was present treated the rich in a different way from the poor but nothing in his letters suggests he did. The conclusion is the same in respect of the educated and uneducated. The uneducated may well have had difficulty in following some of Paul's discussions but he did not deliberately make them complex so that only the learned few would understand. Indeed when in Corinth some boasted of their advanced position in wisdom he was quick to cut them down (1 Cor. 1.18 - 2.16).

Paul's Pharisaic upbringing might have predisposed him to associate only with those who were morally worthy. If so he broke free from this as a Christian. This is not to say that he approved of immoral behavior but that he did not lay down a level of moral attainment for those whom he counted his friends. His Gentile converts were not made immediately pure on conversion; his letters show him fighting time and again to preserve them from falling back into their old ways. Yet he never dissociates himself from them.

The one area however in which Paul is regularly accused of making distinctions between people is that of of sex. He viewed man as the head or origin of woman (1 Cor. 11.3). She stands in the same relation to man as man to Christ. Since there is no equality between man and Christ there can be none between man and woman. Whether Paul wrote Colossians and Ephesians or not there is no reason to suppose that he would have disagreed with what is said in them (see Col. 3.18; Eph. 5.22). Yet there is another side to the matter which comes out in his pastoral work. In his discussion of marriage to the Corinthians there is a careful balancing of husband and wife:

> The husband should give to his wife her conjugal rights, and likewise the wife to her husband. For the wife does not rule over her own body, but the husband does; likewise the husband does not rule over his own body, but the wife does (1 Cor. 7.3,4).

He seems to have had no difficulty in accepting women in the performance of at least some, if not all ministerial functions (1 Cor. 11.5).[36] They prayed and prophesied (preached) and were deacons (Rom. 16.1; the RSV describes Phoebe as a deaconness but the word is masculine in the Greek); there may even have been a female apostle (Rom. 16.7; the original form of the name here was probably feminine, Junia[37]). Did they however preside at the eucharist? We do not know who did in the

Pauline churches. There does not appear to have been a designated official; it was probably the owner of the house in which the congregation met. A woman could have been the owner (Col. 4.15) and presided.[38]

Yet despite such considerations there is a divergence between Paul's theory (Gal. 3.28 puts men and women on the same plane) and his practice in respect of women. We must remember that Paul belonged to a strongly patriarchal society and everything in it would encourage him to sustain male dominance. It is therefore perfectly natural to address his readers as 'brothers' and not as 'brothers and sisters'. 1Thess. 4.3-8 is written entirely from the angle of a male. When we were discussing his attitude to his opponents we observed that while he wrote bitterly against those he did not know he did not do so against those whom he actually knew.[39] It may be that while his cultural conditioning led him to downgrade women when writing about them, when he actually encountered them performing ministerial functions he accepted them.

We have not considered the division between Christian and non-Christian. Would Paul have made a distinction here in his attitude? Such a distinction appears in 1 Pet. 2.17, 'Honor all men. Love the brotherhood'. The later parts of the New Testament stress love within the Christian community rather than love for those outside it (1 Pet. 1.22; 4.8; Heb. 13.1; John 13.34-5; 15.12,17; 1 John 3.23). Yet Jesus taught an equal love for all (Luke 10.25-37; Mark 12.28-34; Matt. 5.43-4). Though there are passages in Paul which suggest he might have followed the tendency of the later New Testament writers along this way (1 Thess. 4.9; Rom. 12.10) there are also those that show he continued the stress of Jesus (Rom. 13.8-10; Gal. 5.14; 1 Thess. 3.12). His letters provide no evidence for his actual behaviour towards outsiders but there is nothing to suggest he made any distinction in his treatment of them.

155

Another point in Paul's theology requires attention. The Christian is free, no longer a slave but a son in the family of God (Gal. 4.1-7). Does Paul treat his converts as free? Paul has at times been accused of telling his converts that they were free of the Torah and immediately imposing on them a new law, that of his own instructions. Theoretically these were not law but did they appear like law to those who heard them? There were times when Paul must have appeared as certain in what he said as the Ten Commandments. If he says he has the mind of Christ, who dare disagree with him? His absoluteness might not have sounded so bad in the ears of his converts if he had allowed that they too might speak to him with the same authority under the Spirit of God. He says that when revelations are being made in a church meeting one prophet should keep quiet to permit another to speak (1 Cor. 14.29-32). Does he display a willingness to keep quiet while others speak to him in the Spirit and instruct him?[40] It must be frankly admitted that Paul allows the parental role here to overcome the reciprocal. The reciprocal would demand that he listen to others as much as they to him. Yet fathers do not often listen to the arguments of their children for they believe they know more. Paul coming from his Jewish background and having had the experience of the Damascus road was convinced it was his place to instruct.

Paul had a very radical view of sin in that he saw it as penetrating every level of being. The flesh, the whole human being, needs to be controlled by the Spirit of God (Rom. 8.1-17; Gal. 5.16-26). Has this happened in Paul's own case? Or to put the question in another way: Does Paul allow sufficiently for the way sin may have corrupted his own thinking and behaviour while he acted as pastor? It is true he was aware that he could fail (Phil. 2.16) but to fail is not the same as to sin. On one occasion he sent a very severe and angry letter to the Corinthians and after it had gone he worried whether it would achieve its intended result. He expressed his relief when it did and the Corinthians repented (2 Cor. 7.5-13). Paul viewed their previous failure as sin from which they needed to repent. The suspicion remains that he did not see the possibility that the sending of his own letter might have been sinful. He seems more worried that it may have been a mistake in tactics.

There is no point where he displays any depth of self-criticism. He is ever ready to criticise his converts, not so ready to permit them to criticise him (1 Cor. 4.3-4). Many would hold that the first pre-requisite of good counselling is the ability of counsellors to look themselves in the face and come to terms with their own fallibility? Paul never leaves the impression that he could have laughed at himself. There is little trace of humour in him.[41] In the days when scholars wrote lives of Jesus they often included a section on his humour. Biographers of Paul never seem to allude to his humour. He could of course show 'wit' through paradox (1 Cor. 1.18-31) and irony (Gal. 6.3; 1 Cor. 6.5; 9.5-7), though the latter could turn into savage sarcasm (1 Cor. 4.8,10; 2 Cor. 11.5, 19). There is nothing of the 'comical' as with Jesus (a camel going through the eye of a needle!).

If Paul displayed no outward consciousness of his own sin or any self-criticism it would be wrong to depict him as an unbending autocrat who having once made up his mind never changed it. There were basic issues in which he did not vary his opinion once he had determined what was right. But in many matters he could be flexible and accomodate himself to others (1 Cor. 9.19-23; 10.33). No one is ever aware of the genuine difficulties which face others who has not himself or herself been through the mill. That Paul can sympathise with the problems facing the weak indicates that he had an understanding of the way sin penetrates the whole human being. Such an attitude then implies an awareness of his own sin. That Paul then does not overtly acknowledge his sin should not lead us to conclude he was unaware of it.

Some compensating factors

If some of this suggests too harsh a judgement on Paul there are a number of general factors to be taken into account which should modify any such harsh conclusion.

If Paul talks to his converts in a way that we might hesitate to do we must remember the difference between his culture and ours. We expect decisions to be taken democratically by general agreement and not unilaterally by one person no matter how eminent. When we find a system other than our own we are prone to judge it harshly from our position and not to make allowances. In the ancient world democracy was either unknown or extremely limited in practice. Most people were used to others making decisions for them. The Hitler youth groups in Germany had strong leadership from above and it was accepted because strong leadership was a feature of their society. The members in the groups did not expect to have to make major decisions. Paul's converts did not expect to be joining a democratic group. They looked for strong leadership. Yet there is only one point at which Paul responds to an accusation of overstrong leadership. It occurs when he assures the Corinthians (2 Cor. 1.24) that he did not seek to lord it over them. The accusation in fact probably did not originate with the Corinthians but with Paul's opponents who were criticising him because they wished to take over the church. 2 Cor. 11.20 shows some of the ways in which those opponents themselves lorded it over his converts. Paul never behaved in those ways. (As a Jew he had physically persecuted Christians; as a Christian his attacks on others are never physical.) That Paul's churches regularly sought his advice shows they accepted his leadership. He says the Galatians were ready to pluck out their eyes for him (4.15; that this was intended metaphorically does not lessen its significance). The Philippians sent money more than once to him after he had left them (Phil. 4.14-16). These are not the attitudes of downtrodden and oppressed converts.

There is no doubt that Paul was a profound thinker but such people do not always suffer fools gladly. They have assumed that what has been perfectly clear and simple to them will be also to their readers. They have not always taken time to give the details of their reasoning but have made their pronouncements and left it at that. It is this which has often made their table-talk so enlivening. It is also true that great thinkers do not always get on easily with others. The qualities that produce intellectual stimulation are not always those that make for good personal relationships. That Paul may have had this difficulty is perhaps hinted at in the way in which when he is emotionally involved his grammar breaks down (e.g. 2 Cor. 7.8; Gal. 2.3). He is also engaged in a perpetual struggle with the culture of the society in which he lived. This may account for the difficulty we have in following his argument in 1 Cor. 11.1-16. He has glimpsed there is something new in Christianity but has not yet been able to free himself from the prevailing culture so as to work out that newness completely.

We should note that he never encouraged a Pauline party. He was as displeased with those in Corinth who claimed to be 'of Paul' as he was those those who claimed to be 'of Peter' (1 Cor. 1.10-17). He did not attempt to win the allegiance of converts to himself but to Christ. At no point does he curry popularity or seek to gain a personal following. He would have condemned out of hand any publicity about himself before he visited a city: 'Come and hear the man who has turned the world upside down'; 'Persecutor turned world evangelist; come and hear what he has to say'. He would instead have bidden his listeners to think only of Christ.

Above all we need to remember what we stressed at the beginning: he had a very different upbringing from the great majority of his converts. He came from the chosen race; they came from paganism. What matters here is not the actual condition of paganism but the way Paul's upbringing had conditioned him to look at it. Objective examination of the ancient world does not suggest that everyone was deeply immersed in sin. Yet Paul took an extremely pessimistic view of contemporary society. We see this in Rom. 1.18-32 where he argues that the rejection of the true God as God leads inevitably to homosexuality and every manner of wickedness. Yet not everyone in the ancient world was a homosexual and there were those in it who condemned homosexuality as strongly as he did. The picture then is over-drawn. The same is true of 1 Thess. 4.4 where he bids Christians take wives for themselves 'in holiness and honour not in the passion of lust like the heathen who do not know God'. Not all in the ancient world married in the passion of lust and it is doubtful if they should be described as not knowing God. But Paul saw the ancient world as a world without light. He believes he himself is transmitting the true light. No wonder there are times when he appears too confident, too absolute. He is the father of his children who has brought them to life. He has therefore the right to instruct and guide them in faith and morals. Had he not done so the Gentile church would never have survived.

For the success of Paul in dealing with his converts we have the testimony of Clement who when he wrote to the Corinthians toward the end of the first century recalled Paul to them (1 Clement 5.5-7; 47.1). It would have been pointless to do this if the memory of Paul in Corinth had gone sour. Whether Acts was written as a response to the publication of Paul's letters or itself led to their publication it shows the honour in which he was held.

We often thank God for Paul the theologian and Paul the missionary pioneer. I believe we can also thank God for Paul the pastor who so demonstrated his care that his churches grew, and left an example so that the church continues to mature.

Notes

1. Cf. p. 17
2. Cf. pp. 29-31
3. But see pp. 86f
4. E.g. F. Milson, *An Introduction to Group Work Skill*, Routledge and Kegan Paul, London & Boston, 1973; R.W. Napier and M.K. Gershenfeld, *Groups: Theory and Experience*, Houghton Mifflin, Boston, 1973.
5. On leadership within the communities see Holmberg, op.cit., pp. 113-123.
6. On Paul's leadership in general see Helen Doohan, *Leadership in Paul* (Good News Studies 11), Michael Glazier, Wilmington, Delaware, 1984, and Holmberg, op.cit., pp. 136-61.
7. Dr and Mrs Howard Taylor, *Hudson Taylor and the China Inland Mission*, China Inland Mission, London, 1940.
8. John Wesley, *Journal*, 2.369-371, quoted in S. Ayling, *John Wesley*, London, Collins, 1979, p.123.
9. R.L. Moore, *John Wesley and Authority: A Psychological Perspective* (AAR Dissertation Series 29), Scholars Press, Missoula, Montana 59806, 1979, p.161.
10. Cf. Ayling, op. cit., p. 175; M. Schmidt, *John Wesley: A Theological Biography* (E.T. by N.P. Goldhawk), Epworth, London, Vol. II, 1971.
11. Cf. Moore, op.cit., pp. 154-5, 161.
12. Cf. Moore, op. cit., p. 160.
13. Cf. Schmidt, op.cit., p. 119.
14. Cf. Moore, op. cit., p. 183.
15. Cf. Ayling, op. cit., pp. 293-4.
16. Cf. Ayling, op.cit., 310.
17. Cf. Schmidt, op.cit., pp. 72-3.
18. Cf. Schmidt, op. cit., pp. 103-4.
19. Cf. Pheme Perkins, *Ministering in the Pauline Churches*, Paulist Press, New York/Ramsey, 1982, pp. 3-7.
20. Cf. pp. 86f
21. See pp. 5f, 18, 22f, 72 *n*. 19, 116

22. See W.M. Ramsay in *Hasting's Dictionary of the Bible*, vol. 3, pp. 368-9.

23. Cf. Allen, op.cit., p. 175.

24. Graham Shaw, op. cit, also claims to make this approach and to judge Paul on Paul's own claims. He finds much to criticise. It is difficult though to see how he moves within Pauline terms when he asserts that Paul was deluded over the resurrection and charismatic gifts. It appears that for Shaw Paul's dogmatism arose from his inner insecurity on these two points (cf. pp. 95,182). But how Shaw knows Paul's inner psychological condition is not made clear.

It is undoubtedly true that there are unpleasant aspects in Paul's writing. But Shaw is too severe. He finds in Paul a 'strident dualism' (p. 165), speaks of puncturing the flow of Paul's rhetoric and asking how he knows certain things to be true (p. 145), instances 'his shrill certainty' (p. 182) and his 'aggressive self-assertion' (p. 183). Yet each of these characteristics could be applied to Shaw's own discussion of Paul. Would it then be wrong to deduce that Shaw's dogmatic assertiveness (I have not been able to discover a single 'probably', 'perhaps' or 'possibly' in all he writes about Paul!) arises out of his own inner insecurity?

25. Cf. p. 48

26. Cf. pp. 109-112

27. See Chapter II.

28. Cf. pp. 18-20

29. Cf. pp. 21, 135

30. See Chapter III.

31. Cf. S.K. Stowers, *The Diatribe and Paul's Letter to the Romans* (SBL Dissertation Series 57), Scholars Press, Chico, California, 1981.

32. Cf. A.J. Malherbe, *Social Aspects of Early Christianity*, Louisiana State University Press, Baton Rouge, 1977, pp.22-7.

33. Petersen, op. cit., p. 295.

34. E.g. see the discussion on maturity, pp. 112, and pp. 129

35. P. Richardson, *Paul's Ethic of Freedom*, Westminster, Philadelphia, 1979, pp. 79-98.

36. If 1 Cor. 14.33b-35 is not a gloss but part of the original letter it lies in line with the divergence in Paul's thinking on women to which we point.

37. See the commentaries on Romans (the R.S.V. translation 'kinsmen', 'men of note' imports masculine terms which are not in the original).

38. Cf. pp. 14f, 141

39. Cf. pp. 121f

40. Cf. Furnish, *Theology and Ethics in Paul*, p. 233.

41. On humour in the New Testament see J.Jonsson, *Humour and Irony in the New Testament*, Brill, Leiden, 1985. Pp. 223-42 treat Paul.

SUBJECT INDEX

AUTHOR INDEX

167

INDEX OF SCRIPTURE AND OTHER REFERENCES